The Politics of Scarcity

The Politics of Scarcity

Resource Conflicts in International Relations

PHILIP CONNELLY
AND
ROBERT PERLMAN

Published for
THE ROYAL INSTITUTE OF
INTERNATIONAL AFFAIRS
by
OXFORD UNIVERSITY PRESS
LONDON   NEW YORK   TORONTO
1975

Oxford University Press, Ely House, London W.1

GLASGOW NEW YORK TORONTO MELBOURNE WELLINGTON
CAPE TOWN IBADAN NAIROBI DAR ES SALAAM LUSAKA ADDIS ABABA
DELHI BOMBAY CALCUTTA MADRAS KARACHI LAHORE DACCA
KUALA LUMPUR SINGAPORE HONG KONG TOKYO

ISBN 0 19 218308 7

Printed in Great Britain by
Hazell Watson & Viney Ltd, Aylesbury, Bucks

Foreword by Andrew Shonfield

The origins of this volume go back to some discussions held at Chatham House in the first half of 1972. We were concerned at that stage that we had not sufficiently explored the long-term consequences of the change in the ownership and control of natural resources following on the end of the colonial era. We suspected that the apparent quiescence of the primary producing nations, who indeed complained about their adverse terms of trade for the products which they sold to the developed countries but were consistently and easily defeated in the actual process of bargaining, might well disguise a more general delayed-action effect. It was probable that it would take time before the underlying mood and the assumptions that went with colonialism, most especially the assumption of ultimate powerlessness in a clash of interests with the advanced industrial nations of the Western world, would be eliminated.

It so happened that our questionings on this topic occurred at a time when the issue of the economics of resource scarcity was coming strongly into vogue. It is hard to remember precisely, but it may have been that the general debate about long-term scarcities as a constraint on world economic growth nudged us into a greater sense of urgency in pursuing our problem. It was at any rate clear that the prospect of a change in international relations brought about by a more assertive policy on the part of the resource owners in the less developed world would be considerably reinforced by the sense of impending shortages—whether this last was in fact justified or not.

We decided to focus our attention on *non-renewable resources*, not because the larger issue of primary produce at large lacked interest, but, more practically, because we were anxious to limit the discussion to something which appeared to be a manageable area of discussion and research. We were looking for hard cases in which the clear prospect of the ultimate exhaustion of a finite resource producing the major revenue of a less developed country was likely to be a dominant factor in shaping its relations with the rich industrial nations of the West, where the main locus of political power in the international system had rested for the past couple of hundred years. Our aim was to discover what kind of power absolute local control over this kind of natural resource might bring in the post-colonial era, and how the international system as a whole, including the resource-poor nations of the developing world, could adapt to it. We put these ideas to the managers of some of the international companies operating in the minerals field and we were interested to discover that, although they were of course thinking about them, they had apparently been inclined to analyse the problems involved in a somewhat compartmentalized fashion. In particular, the metals producers looked at the matter in terms of the specific conditions of the mining and transport of their products and the oil producers in terms of theirs. One of the first useful results of this enterprise was therefore to induce the oil-men and the metals-men to examine the problem in a common framework of analysis. The framework was provided by the study of international relations in their economic and political dimensions. Our data was as much economic as political, though our ultimate objective was to arrive at a political judgement of the new situation on the basis of economic analysis.

To this end Chatham House assembled a Study Group, on which I served as chairman, from the autumn of 1972 until early 1974. The main group which held nine meetings consisted of a number of people with direct responsibility for policy-making in the top management of companies and in government, plus some academic experts concerned with international politics and economics, strategy, and technology. We discovered, however, that this rather high-powered group did not always come successfully to grips with the issues emerging out of the detail of particular national and other interests operating in different regions of the world. A number of *ad hoc* regional sub-groups were therefore formed, drawing on the deeper knowledge of specialists in the politics and economics of those areas to guide the deliberations of the main group. We gave our attention to three regions in particular—Latin America, South Asia, and the Middle East. It will be understood that many of those involved in the different phases of this operation, numbering some 40 to 45 people, would not, in view of the positions which they held, have felt able to assist us if their contributions had not been covered by the familiar Chatham House confidentiality rule. It therefore seemed best to apply the principle of anonymity to the membership of all these study groups. It would have been misleading to the reader to have provided the names of some of those who were involved and not others.

However, the book itself has nothing anonymous about it. It is the expression of the views of the two authors, Philip Connelly and Robert Perlman, who have consulted the Chatham House group at every stage, have presented papers to it, argued with it, but have in the end made up their own minds. Their labours were first interrupted and then protracted by the outbreak of the Arab-Israeli War in the autumn of 1973 and its aftermath. These events gave a violently topical twist to the whole exercise. Indeed, the problem for the authors and for Chatham House at that stage was how to avoid becoming *too* topical. The winter of 1973/74 did not provide the ideal atmosphere for a cool appraisal of the long-term perspective on the rôle of oil and other minerals in the system of international relations. It would be idle to pretend that the views of either the authors or the members of the study group were affected in no particular by the experience of those anxious months, when the evidence about the limits to which the participants in the conflict over our oil supplies were willing to go, shifted and changed sharply sometimes from day to day. But I think it is true to say that the broad framework of this study, which had already been established before the crisis, stood up rather well to the unexpectedly early test of events of the kind that we had tried to foresee.

29 April 1974   A. S.

Contents

P.S.—1*

Figures

Tables

Acknowledgements

More people have contributed to the making of this book than space permits us to record. The main debt of gratitude is owed to the members of the Chatham House Study Group on 'Resources in International Policy'. In addition, many people in the resource industries, in academic life and elsewhere were drawn in to clarify particular aspects of the subject. Individual staff members of several major companies were particularly helpful in supplying data, in discussing the content of the book with us and in reviewing sections of the text in draft.

Special thanks are due to three members of Commodities Research Unit, Robin Adams, Nigel Greenwood, and Anthony Murray, for their contributions to sections of the Anatomy of Scarcity. The section on the Organisation of Petroleum Exporting Countries (OPEC) in Chapter 5 draws heavily upon the expertise of Jeanne Connelly, to whom much else besides is owed. If the end product of our study possesses any shape at all, this is largely due to commentary on our final drafts by Ian Smart, the Deputy Director of Chatham House, and to the editorial assistance of Ann-Margaret Willis and of Judith Gurney at Chatham House.

We are very conscious that, in aiming at a moving target from a moving platform, our views on this complex subject are unlikely to coincide with those of our many helpers. With more than the normal fervour, therefore, we absolve from responsibility all others, including the institutions to which we are affiliated.

Philip Connelly
Robert Perlman

Abbreviations

CIPEC	Conseil Intergouvernmental des Pays Exportateurs de Cuivre
COMECON	Council for Mutual Economic Aid
GDP	Gross domestic product
GNP	Gross national product
IBA	International Bauxite Association
IMF	International Monetary Fund
IPC	Iraq Petroleum Company Ltd
LDC	Less developed country
LME	London Metal Exchange
OAPEC	Organisation of Arab Petroleum Exporting Countries
OECD	Organisation for Economic Co-operation and Development
OPEC	Organisation of Petroleum Exporting Countries
RDLDC	Resource deficient less developed country
UNCTAD	United Nations Conference on Trade & Development
UNDP	United Nations Development Programme

1 Introduction

This book deals with the anatomy and the politics of scarcity. Several viewpoints are needed to make sense out of what is happening to the world's non-renewable natural resources. The perceptions of the economist must be brought to bear on the behaviour of commodities which are both finite and a fundamental component of world trade and investment. The political scientist soon recognizes the central rôle played in resource transactions by such familiar conceptual tools as dependence and interdependence, sovereignty, ownership, and bargaining power. So wide is the impact of resources on international affairs that the talents of the historian, engineer, and many others could well be deployed to add further dimensions of relevance to the analysis. In that sense, what follows is, as much as anything, an agenda for research. But time is not on our side. For the international community, the decade ahead will be crowded with complex and far-reaching policy choices centred on resources; indeed the process has already started, with oil. The importance of establishing the right framework for these choices is some justification for attempting to cover so intricate a subject in this brief essay.

The quickening pace of change in the field of resources, and the coalition of international economics and politics, can well be illustrated at the start by two recent snapshot views of the oil industry.

In 1970, the average revenue per barrel of Gulf crude obtained by the governments of the Gulf oil-producing states stood at around 90 U.S. cents. Total revenues of countries in OPEC (Organisation of Petroleum Exporting Countries) in that year amounted to around $7 billion. Virtually all crude oil produced in OPEC countries was in the hands of the American and European oil industry and the governments of the oil-consuming areas were content to leave all facets of their oil supply policy in those hands. Oil was not an issue in the politics of the European Community or the Atlantic Alliance. In Saudi Arabia, the oil industry, in the shape of the 100 per cent U.S.-owned Aramco Consortium, was considering first outline plans to triple production from 3·5 million barrels per day to 10 million barrels per day in 1977, a level which appeared essential to meet burgeoning oil demand, growing at 7 per cent per annum. That growth rate, amongst others, was beginning to attract the attention of some academics who were to be assured of a receptive audience when they published their assertion that the essential decision for the resource consuming countries was unilaterally to moderate the growth of their consumption before natural processes of depletion, pollution, and population increase brought it—with much else—to a disastrous halt.

Only four years later, the picture is totally different. Following an Arab-Israeli war in which Arab oil producers in unison deployed the 'oil weapon' of production cuts and destination embargoes and, thus unified, unilaterally increased crude prices fourfold, Gulf crude is netting the producer governments over $9 per barrel. OPEC revenues are running at about $120 billion per annum and those OPEC governments who in 1973 agreed to 25 per cent participation in oil production operations, currently have 60 per cent and are now actively contemplating 100 per cent control. The French and British Governments have concluded separate bilateral oil supply deals with oil producing states outside the normal framework of the oil industry and have announced their intention to seek others. Protests from other members of the European Community and from the United States have accompanied these bilateral deals although some of the former were not slow to copy the idea. Oil policy has assumed a centre stage position in the politics of the European Community and United States/West European relations have declined abysmally for a period, mainly over the same issue. Saudi crude production stood at 7·5 million barrels per day in February 1974, against a level previously planned by Aramco for that month of 9·3 million barrels per day; and considerable uncertainty was being felt amongst responsible observers as to whether production would ever attain the 20 million barrels per day which had been nominated as the new production target for 1980 necessary to meet pre-Middle East war projections of free world crude supply and demand. In a world of depressed oil demand and quadrupled prices, preoccupations with oil depletion problems have tended to be set aside.

These highlights of the oil story in two recent and shortly separated years provide a particularly dramatic example of how radical and sudden changes can take place in the arena of natural resources and how deeply they can engage wider international political issues. Oil and the other energy fuels are indeed central to any discussion of resources and they will figure largely in the account which follows; but this is not a book solely about oil. We have set out to enlarge the terms of the recent debate about non-renewable natural resources by reviewing and analysing the broader questions in international relations posed or sharpened by developments in the consumption and ownership of resources in a period roughly defined as up to the end of the century. Our theme is that there is a dynamic process at work in this area which cannot fully be classified in the categories of either economic or political analysis taken in isolation. The rest of this book is an attempt to describe that process and its implications. It could be described, very generally, as follows.

As economic growth continues, advanced industrial resource-importing nations are becoming more dependent on less developed resource-exporting countries (Europe, for example, on copper from Zambia and Chile; Japan on oil from the Middle East). Some major importers (such as the United States) are also significant owners of at least some resources, while others such as Japan are almost completely dependent on imports for all resources. In general terms, however, a set of reciprocal relationships is emerging between industrialized importers and less developed exporters such that the increasing dependence of the former is reflected to varying degrees in the increasing bargaining strength of the latter (who in many cases will recently have assumed resource ownership following a colonial period). But the world is not polarized into those two camps. There are at least two other differently situated groups of international actors who will watch the resource dependency situation with interest.

There is firstly a disparate group of relatively developed nations (the Soviet Union, China, Australia, Canada) whose self-sufficiency or super-sufficiency in many resources offers them both insulation from the increasing political and economic pressures of dependence and also the option of acting to advance their own interests in a situation created by the imposition of such pressures on others. Then there are those less developed nations such as India which do not possess adequate natural resources for their own needs or at any rate lack the means or opportunity of exploiting those they have, and which require to import many raw materials. The new dimensions for political analysis arise from the matrix of interactions between the four groupings in this quadrilateral: developing exporters, developed and developing importers, and the self-sufficient.

The strength of resource dependency relationships is modified by, and expressed through, several processes: the location, costs and lead times of substitute materials; the availability of capital to invest in substitute resources; the varying balance of payments effects of a change in the terms of trade in favour of actual or potential resource exporters; the effect of price increases in rationing resource demand and bringing substitutes into play; the institutional arrangements surrounding supply and demand; the desire to preserve the environment; the intensity of non-economic political objectives, and so on. The basic perspective of this study, therefore, stresses what are primarily international political concepts of changing resource ownership and dependence; but we attempt to sharpen the discussion by dealing simultaneously with the interactive effect on politics of economic factors such as depletion, substitution, costs, and flows of funds.

We have found it necessary to be selective in our examination of resources. No account is taken of developments in agricultural resources on the ground that they are, at least in principle, renewable. On the other hand, it has become clear that developments in the consumption and ownership of energy resources, especially oil, give rise to an array of problems of particular importance and complexity, having a bearing on many international issues. The subject of energy has therefore been given extended analysis.

Resource-based issues will have an impact on the framework of international politics by reviving old problems to which old solutions may no longer be appropriate, by highlighting or modifying current problems and their means of resolution and by creating entirely new problems requiring new solutions. Colonial times provide an example of the first category. Although rich nations often obtained access to raw materials in their colonies in completely peaceful circumstances, it was always open to them to retain access by force of arms. It is generally held that, nowadays, overt military solutions to resource supply problems are unlikely to be sought by rich resource consuming countries against recalcitrant, less developed resource exporters. Alternative means of resolving such conflicts have to be sought. And yet this position has not escaped questioning during the 1973/74 Arab oil production cuts and embargoes.

The vast bulk of fuel and mineral trade and consumption has taken place without direct dealings between one nation and another, owing to the operation in this area, especially since the Second World War, of large international corporations. Given the importance to both the consuming and producing economies of the commodities developed and traded by these companies, few analyses of international political institutions in recent years have failed to include some reference to their activities and the issues raised thereby, particularly their alleged challenge to the sovereignty of governments. Yet here again the recent history of 'participation' in the oil industry, of OPEC pricing policy decisions and of British and French 'oil diplomacy' must qualify the thesis that the power of international corporations is steadily increasing. This is one example of an area of current debate which will certainly be enlarged, and we hope may be clarified, in the perspective provided by international resource problems.

Yet another, and much more pressing, enhancement of a current tension in the world order is the severe effect on less developed nations without adequate raw material endowments of sharply increased import prices for commodities like oil, essential for their economic development.

In recent times the best-known public and systematic treatment of allegedly new world problems posed by resource depletion has been the work conducted at the Massachusetts Institute of Technology (MIT) for the Club of Rome and described in *The Limits to Growth* by Dennis Meadows *et al.* (1972). This study has had a major influence on the terms of the modern debate about resources. Its primary focus was to use the technique of systems dynamics to demonstrate a point of principle—subsequently hotly disputed—that continued world economic growth could not be sustained much beyond the end of the century. This was held to be due to the operation of a number of constraints depicted in their mathematical model of the world economic system: pollution, availability of arable land, etc. The depletion of non-renewable natural resources formed one such constraint. The solution advocated was a non-growth state of global equilibrium. The resources subsector of the model has been criticized for failing to take adequate account of the operation of the price mechanism, and of research and development, in increasing the effective reserves of resources.[1] Nor did the analysis in *The Limits to Growth* in any way discuss the politics of resource ownership, an omission which reflected the highly aggregated nature of the model—no interactions were represented between different geographical areas. In contrast, we hope to show that the resource challenge to international policy-makers is primarily that of re-adjusting the relationships between nations, and only secondarily the problems of growth and depletion.

The purpose of this study is, then, to describe the broad analytical framework of facts, processes, and actors and to set out in a constructive way the policy options raised for the international community in their dealings with one another by an emergent complex of problems centred upon the consumption and ownership of resources. Part I—'The anatomy of scarcity'—provides in Chapters 2, 3, and 4, an overview of the nature of resources and the special problem of energy, and the economic mechanisms with which they are associated. The analysis continues in Part II—'The politics of scarcity'—by identifying the situation and objectives of each of the four main groupings: the resource exporting developing nations (Chapter 5); the resource importing industrial nations (Chapter 6); the resource self-sufficient nations (Chapter 7); the resource poor developing nations (Chapter 8).

Chapter 9 discusses the implications for economic and political policies of the interaction of the interests of these main actors in the resource arena.

It is clear that this subject-matter could be arranged for examination in many alternative ways. The numerous cross-connections between different parts of the problem make any one system of classification incomplete or unsatisfactory from certain points of view. In particular, an alternative scheme could have been one focused upon individual resources or groups of resources. However, given some special descriptive material on energy, the core of the subsequent discussion on geo-political issues lends itself more appropriately to an aggregated geographical framework—the framework of the resource quadrilateral.

Note

1. See H. S. D. Cole, *et. al.*, eds, *Thinking about the Future*, Science Policy Research Unit, University of Sussex, 1973.

Part One
The Anatomy of Scarcity

2 What are resources?

For purposes of this book the term resources is used to mean natural resources excluding renewable animal and vegetable resources. In other words, we are concerned with non-renewable minerals such as oil, coal, iron, and copper. This category can be subdivided into those resources which can be recycled to a greater or lesser extent (including most of the metals) and those which are apparently destroyed when they are consumed (the most notable example being fuels). For ease of reference, concise economic profiles of the major resources considered are listed in Appendix A.

Recycled material (scrap) is a major source of several important metals: about 20 per cent, 35 per cent, and 40 per cent of the world production of aluminium, steel, and copper, respectively, derives from recycled scrap; in the case of lead, the proportion is even higher. These percentages can theoretically be raised; an increased investment in reclamation technology is one of the policy options open to industrialized consumers of raw materials (see Chapter 4). In this chapter, however, we concentrate on primary demand for, and supply of, metals.

In speaking of the availability of resources, a distinction has to be made between known reserves and theoretical abundance. The abundance of a mineral is the total content of the particular mineral in the earth's crust or in the oceans. Widely-accepted estimates of abundance have been made on the basis of geological research, being normally inferred from an analysis of samples taken in the first mile of the earth's crust. In the case of fossil fuels, however, there are no such widely-accepted figures for abundance. Reserves, or known reserves, are occurrences of minerals that have actually been discovered. A certain proportion of these reserves is economically recoverable under current conditions. Indeed they may sometimes be the proven reserves of existing mines. On the other hand, they may not be recoverable at current prices using current technology. The concept of reserves thus tends to be somewhat elastic: estimates can increase as prices rise or as technical changes appear to be imminent. However, minerals in concentrations that are, or might in the medium term become, commercially viable are here included under the heading of 'reserves'.

Table 2.1 sets out the value of world consumption of four broad categories of mineral resources: energy resources, ferrous minerals (including alloys and constituents of steel as well as iron itself), non-ferrous metals, and, finally, non-metallic industrial minerals. The figures refer to 1968, although the values are expressed in terms of 1973 dollars.

Table 2.1. *Value of World Consumption of Mineral Resources by Group, 1968*
(*billions of 1973 dollars*)

	U.S.	% of GNP	Rest of world	% of GNP*	Total	% of GNP*
Energy	24·3	2·3	40·0	1·6	64·3	1·9
Ferrous	7·3	0·7	28·0	1·1	35·3	1·0
Non-ferrous	6·3	0·6	17·9	0·8	24·2	0·7
Non-metallic	7·5	0·7	30·9	1·2	38·4	1·1
Total	45·4	4·3	116·8	4·7	162·2	4·6

* Commodities Research Unit estimate.

Source: U.S. Bureau of Mines, *Mineral Facts and Problems, 1970* (adjusted to include value of pig iron production).

Table 2.2 gives a more detailed breakdown of consumption of major minerals. It is interesting to note that, outside the energy sector, only iron, sand, gravel, and stone, copper and aluminium account, by themselves, for significantly more than 1 per cent of the world's total mineral consumption. This table does contain a certain amount of double-counting because energy is consumed in the production of minerals, especially metals that must be smelted and refined. Thus the cost of this energy consumption enters into the value of metal produced. However, this effect is unlikely to over-state the total by more than 10 per cent, and has been allowed for in the case of iron.

To put these figures into perspective, we have expressed consumption of the various resource groups in Table 2.1 as a percentage of gross national product (GNP). Consumption of mineral resources

Table 2.2. *World Primary Consumption of Major Mineral Resources, 1968 and 1972*
(million tonnes; billions of 1973 dollars)

	1968			1972	
	Quantity	*Value*	*% of total value*	*Quantity*	*Value*
Energy					
Oil	1,968	38·73	23·9	2,590	48·60ᵉ
Natural gas*	29·7	5·96	3·7	40·5	8·12ᵉ
Coal	2,187	14·76	9·1 ⎫	2,660	20·0ᵉ
Peat	221	3·16	2·0 ⎭		
Ferrous					
Iron†	381	32·20	19·9	455ᵉ	41·00ᵉ
Nickel	0·49	1·25	0·8	0·56	1·87
Non-ferrous					
Aluminium	8·8	6·07	3·7	11·5	6·87
Copper	5·3	7·68	4·7	6·8	7·43
Lead	3·1	1·14	0·7	3·7	1·18
Zinc	4·9	1·79	1·1	5·4	2·16
Non-metallic					
Chlorine	17·1	1·66	1·0 ⎫		
Clay	317	1·85	1·1 ⎪		
Sand, gravel, and stone‡	11·3	22·19	13·7 ⎬	n.a.	
Titanium (excl. metallic uses)	1·3	1·48	0·9 ⎭		
Total of above minerals	n.a.	139·92	863		
TOTAL	n.a.	162·20	100·0		

* Quantities in units of 10^{12} cu. ft   † Pig iron.   ‡ Quantities in billions of tonnes.   e Estimate.

Sources: U.S. Bureau of Mines, *Mineral Facts and Problems, 1970; World Bureau of Metal Statistics, 1973*; Metallgesellschaft, *Metal Statistics,* 1973; American Metal Market, *Metal Statistics, 1972; American Bureau of Metal Statistics Yearbook, 1972.*

only accounts for 4·3 per cent of the total value of the United States output of goods and services, over half of this relatively small figure being attributable to energy resources. In other words, about 4 per cent of the productive effort of the United States economy is devoted —either directly or through the medium of international trade—to extracting minerals from the ground and transforming them into commercially useful, standardized commodities, such as refined metal ingots and petrol. This is a very small proportion of total GNP. Why, then, is so much attention currently paid to potential problems in such a relatively unimportant sector of the economy?

The answer is, of course, that fuels and minerals permeate every aspect of economic activity. Man—or economic man, at any rate— is primarily a transformer rather than a creator, and the economic process is essentially one of transforming inputs into increasingly useful (and hence valuable) outputs. The importance of natural resources lies in the fact that they provide both the raw material which is transformed and the energy without which the transformation cannot take place. To understand the resource problem, it is therefore necessary to analyse the useful properties which the different mineral resources embody.

The demand for almost all mineral resources is a derived one: that is, a fundamental demand for some property—strength, say, or electrical conductivity—underlies the demand for them. The fact that most properties are shared by several minerals gives rise to the possibility of substitution, and is the prime reason for being suspicious of simple extrapolations into the future of past consumption of particular resources. Whereas it may yield a good first approximation to project a long-term trend of total energy demand forward to the year 2000, it is more questionable to apply the same technique to the specific consumption of oil or coal. Thus, it is not the demand for individual resources that we should be concerned about but the demand for the properties they contain.

The principal properties which can make a particular metal valuable are strength, lightness, electrical conductivity, thermal conductivity, corrosion resistance, malleability, and ductility; while the valuable properties of non-metallic minerals include energy-content (by far the most important property) and a host of specialized chemical uses based on the composition of the mineral. In addition, many minerals which are of little value by themselves are valuable because they are inputs into the production of metals possessing some of the properties listed above. Examples of these secondary minerals include nickel in stainless steel, manganese in virtually all steel (giving the steel added malleability), and fluorspar (in the form of cryolite) in the electrolytic reduction of alumina to aluminium.

The properties mentioned above are often required jointly: for example, lightness is a highly prized quality when found in conjunction with strength or conductivity, or both. The rapid growth (about 9 per cent per annum) in aluminium consumption since

World War II is undoubtedly due largely to its combination of these useful properties: its lightness makes it preferable to steel in many structural applications, while the same property—lightness—has led to an almost complete substitution of aluminium for copper in over-head electrical transmission lines. Two of the desirable properties listed for metals, ductility and malleability, are only useful in con-junction with other properties, and are of no use in their own: they are desired simply because they extend the range of shapes and sizes a particular metal can be made to assume.

As with metals, so with fuels—oil, gas, coal, and peat: it is not the materials that are required *per se* but the property they possess of combustibility enabling them to release energy for use in heating, lighting, transport, etc. In talking of energy, it is normal to distin-guish between different sources of energy. The energy resources or fuels listed above constitute 'primary' energy, but often they need to be transformed into 'secondary' energy such as electricity before they can be applied conveniently for the purposes of mankind.

Pessimists and Optimists

In the current debate about the world's consumption of non-renewable mineral resources, most commentators and analysts have tended to fall into one or two opposed camps: the pessimists and the optimists. They differ not so much on the statistics of consumption and reserves as on the interpretation that should be given to them. Table 2.3 shows currently known reserves and estimates the 'life' of these reserves on two assumptions: one that consumption is held at its current level; and the other that consumption increases at a rate similar to that in the recent past. The table also shows the theoretical abundance of each resource in the first mile of the earth's crust and relates this to known reserves.

The simplest version of the pessimistic view is that exponential growth (i.e. growth at a constant percentage rate per annum) in the consumption of certain basic non-renewable resources—in parti-cular, fossil fuels and metals—will soon exhaust this planet's reserves. If it is accepted both that the growth rate of consumption is exponential and that the reserves of these mineral resources are fixed, it follows as a matter of simple arithmetic that reserves will eventually run out. Indeed, the statistics in Table 2.3 show that this could happen quite soon in some cases.

This thesis, which underlay the natural resources section of the Club of Rome's *Limits to Growth* (Meadows, *et al.*) and has been

Table 2.3. *Reserves and Ultimate Abundance of Metals, 1973*
(tonnes)

	Known reserves (tonnes)	Life of reserves at current consumption rates* (years)	Life of reserves allowing for trend growth-rate in consumption* (years)	Total abundance in oceans (tonnes)	Total abundance in first mile of earth's crust (under dry land only) (tonnes)	Total abundance as a multiple of known reserves
Aluminium	1.2×10^9	100	31	1.6×10^{10}	5.4×10^{16}	$>$ 10 Million
Copper	3.1×10^8	36	21	4.7×10^9	4.6×10^{13}	
Iron	1.1×10^{11}	240	93	1.2×10^{10}	3.3×10^{16}	$>$100 Thousand
Lead	9.1×10^7	26	21	4.7×10^8	1.1×10^{13}	
Mercury	1.1×10^6	13	13	4.7×10^7	3.3×10^{11}	
Nickel	6.6×10^7	150	53	3.1×10^9	5.3×10^{13}	
Tin	4.4×10^6	17	15	4.7×10^9	2.6×10^{13}	$>$ 1 Million
Zinc	1.1×10^8	23	18	1.6×10^{10}	8.7×10^{13}	$>$100 Thousand

*Taken from D. H. Meadows, *et al*., *The Limits to Growth*.

Sources: U.S. Bureau of Mines, *Commodity Statements 1973*: J. L. Mero, 'Oceanic Mineral Resources', in *Futures* 1, 2, 1968; Crustal abundance derived from *Encyclopaedia Britannica*, 1973, art. 'Geochemistry'.

adopted by conservationist and other writers, has the merit of dramatizing the quantitative implications of compound growth. For example, doubling the assumed reserves of a resource does not increase its life to anything like the same extent. If there are forty years' worth of some metal ore left in the ground and consumption of the metal is increasing at 7 per cent per annum (doubling every 10 years), a sudden doubling of available resources would only increase their 'life' by 10 years, i.e. 25 per cent.

A more subtle type of pessimism is displayed by analysts who acknowledge that there are various 'feedback' mechanisms linking scarcity to consumption, but question whether the large consuming economies will be able to adapt their consumption pattern quickly enough to obviate the more unpleasant consequences of resource scarcity. It is true, they say, that actual or impending scarcity of particular resources will lead to price rises and consequent incentives to make economies in consumption and to substitute plentiful resources for scarce ones. However, it is not at all obvious that an advanced, complex economy, consuming mineral resources in every industrial sector—either directly, or indirectly through these sectors' purchases of mineral based inputs from other sectors—will necessarily adapt to a rapidly changing situation in the optimum manner. This argument is developed at greater length in Chapter 4

A third, and milder, form of pessimism accepts that the price mechanism will efficiently ration increasingly scarce minerals, but points out that more real resources will be absorbed by the extractive sector as ore-grades fall, with a consequent fall (or slower rise) in real income as relatively fewer goods and services can be produced. This view, based as it is on the assumption of rising costs, may be termed the Ricardian approach, as opposed to the Club of Rome's Malthusian approach, which assumes that mineral reserves are fixed.

On the opposite side of the debate, there are two different types of optimistic views about mineral reserves, both of which rely on the efficiency of economic mechanisms. The first argues that impending shortages generate rising prices, which in turn act as danger signals, discouraging the use of scarce minerals and stimulating the use of cheaper ones. In this view, there will always be enough minerals to go round—at a price. But that final rider is, of course, extremely important, since the economic welfare of the consuming economies may be seriously impaired if a large proportion of their capital and labour must be devoted merely to obtaining raw materials.

The second optimistic argument is more unequivocal than the

first. It maintains that man is sufficiently adaptable and (literally) resourceful in his extraction and consumption of minerals to counteract any possible effects of scarcity. Substitution, recycling, and new technology (both in mining and in the use of materials) are the weapons most frequently invoked to ward off the evil spirits of resource depletion. In addition, it is pointed out that reserves are not fixed, since high prices stimulate exploration and since technical advances can increase resources quite suddenly by making some previously worthless mineral valuable.

The first step towards an objective view of resource depletion must be to dismiss the notion of absolute (Malthusian) scarcity. The figures in Table 2.3 show that actual abundance of minerals is many thousands, indeed in most cases many millions, of times greater than known reserves. Physical availability in the earth's crust and under its oceans is not therefore a crucial constraint. This generalization does not, admittedly, apply to fossil and mineral fuels, some of which are much less abundant than metals. The special case of fuels is therefore discussed in detail in Chapter 3. For the present, however, as far as metals are concerned, the problem is clearly a technical and economic one: how to discover and extract the metals at something less than a prohibitive cost in terms of the world economy.

Economic scarcity of mineral resources implies a Ricardian view: although reserves are so large as to be practically infinite, the argument goes, the real cost of extracting mineral resources will rise as the high-grade, easily accessible deposits are depleted. The standard rejoinder to this line of reasoning is that advances in technology can keep pace with, and possibly outrun, the decrease in ore grades. Evidence can be adduced to support both arguments.

H. J. Barnett and C. Morse, in their theoretical and empirical analysis of resource scarcity entitled *Scarcity and Growth* (1963), used several criteria—including costs per unit of extracted minerals and the proportion of the labour force in the extractive sector—in their examination of the hypothesis of Ricardian scarcity. Broadly, their conclusion was that unit costs in the U.S. had decreased significantly over the 75-year period (1880–1955) which they considered, and that the proportion of the labour force in the extractive sector had fallen markedly—from 56 per cent to 14 per cent. This conclusion is partially supported by analysis of individual commodity prices: Figure 1 shows trends in the real cost of pig iron, copper, and aluminium, the three most important metals in terms of the value of annual consumption. The real price (i.e. the current price deflated

by the U.S. wholesale price index) of iron has remained fairly constant since World War II, while that of aluminium shows an overall
downward trend. In the case of copper, however, there seems little
doubt that technology has not succeeded in keeping down its real
price. The large fluctuations in the price of copper compared to that
of aluminium reflect the influence of stable producer pricing of

Fig. 1: Real Price of Pig Iron, Copper, and Aluminium, 1920–38
and 1950–72. Semi Logarithmic Scale, 1957–59=100.*

* Current price deflated by U.S. wholesale price index (1957–59=100).
† London Metal Exchange.
Source : Commodities Research Unit.

aluminium as contrasted with the free-market pricing of copper; it
does not affect the present argument. It is, moreover, a vindication of
the optimistic view that steel and aluminium have invaded several
structural, mechanical, and electrical applications formerly the
preserve of copper.

There is a danger of being lulled into complacency by the rhetoric
of extrapolation. At least in the absence of more solid information,

optimistic projections of past decreases in real costs have as little
foundation as pessimistic projections of past increases in consumption. It must be shown, first, that technology can cope with the ever
larger tonnages of ore which need to be extracted and refined and,
second, that large new deposits will continue to be found in the future.

Technology and Technique

As regards technology, it is worth making a distinction between
fundamental changes in the technology of mining, smelting, etc., on
the one hand, and gradual improvements in the techniques of
design, mechanical efficiency, etc. within a given technology, on the
other. For convenience, we refer to the first as technological progress
and to the second as technical progress. This distinction is not
merely a scholastic one; there are usually physical or theoretical
limits to technical improvements, whereas projections of technological progress, as defined above, are more speculative. To take
an example, the basic technology of mining was revolutionized
when open-pit mining commenced on a large scale towards the turn
of the century, making for capital-intensive methods of production
which economized on labour. (Interestingly, the fortuitous nature of
this type of progress is shown by the fact that the mechanical engineering advances which underlay this change came about as a result
of methods used in digging the Panama Canal.) Since the open-pit
revolution, however, no changes in basic technology have occurred,
but technical improvements have steadily enabled economies of
scale to be reaped. Further technical progress within the existing
technology appears possible, although some mining engineers point
out that there are diseconomies of scale due to the uncoordinated
growth in the size of trucks and drag-lines. More important in the
long run is likely to be the environmental impact of ever larger open-
pit mines, including both public opposition to 'unpleasant' mining
operations and possible legal requirements for the restraint of
pollution and restoration of the land after operations cease. Even
stronger political and ecological objections apply, however, to the
next technological step: nuclear mining.

   Another example of the distinction between technical and technological progress is provided by the aluminium industry. The
world's entire supply of primary aluminium is currently produced by
the Bayer-Hall process, which has not been changed in any fundamental respect for 80 years. In this process, bauxite is converted to
alumina, which is then reduced electrolytically to pure aluminium.

Continual technical advances have been made within this technology, by economizing on raw materials such as cryolite and aluminium fluoride, increasing the size of the electrolytic pots, etc. Recently, however, largely prompted by increases in energy cost, technological progress has been reflected in two new processes patented by Alcoa and Applied Aluminium Research Corporation in the United States. The latter (the Toth process) is claimed to economize greatly on energy since it uses fuel directly (in much the same way as a blast furnace uses coking coal) instead of indirectly, through electricity. However, even the Alcoa process, which still uses electrolysis, is said to use 20 per cent less energy than the Bayer-Hall process. In addition, these new technologies are important from the point of view of possible depletion of bauxite, since they can use certain non-bauxitic and more abundant aluminiferous clays as a raw material.

The second requirement for the future—the discovery of large new deposits—is more difficult to analyse. It was shown above (see Table 2.3) that many billions of tonnes of the major metals exist in the first mile of the earth's crust and on the ocean floor. The tonnages were based on geological analyses of the composition of the earth's surface. However, the figures offer no guide as to where these tonnages may be found and how evenly distributed they are. The latter point is important, because the optimistic answer to Ricardian scarcity is that gradual improvements in technology will match (or outstrip) gradual reductions in ore grades. But are ore grades likely to fall gradually? There is a well-known relationship called by economic geologists the Lasky ratio after its original formulator.[1] This formula, based originally on particular deposits of porphyry copper, states that the average ore grade falls arithmetically as the total tonnage of ore (not metal) increases geometrically. Lasky found that, on average, the tonnage of ore increased by some 18 per cent for every drop of 0·1 per cent in ore grade. The arithmetic/ geometric relationship does not imply that total contained metal increases as ore grade falls: in the deposits analysed by Lasky (which contained grades ranging from 2 per cent to zero) most of the copper was contained in ore grading 0·5 per cent and higher, while over half of the total copper was in ore containing more than 0·9 per cent copper. But these relationships are only likely to hold for particular deposits: there is no reason to suppose that they apply to total world reserves. The geological evidence does not suggest that there is any smooth gradation in ore grades, such as that suggested by the Lasky formula, from rich ores to rock containing only a few parts per million of metal. The true picture is likely to be one of a relatively small number of quite rich deposits and an enormous tonnage of rock containing small traces of metal—without much in between. The critical question, then, is: how close are we to running out of relatively rich deposits?

We have so far said nothing about the rate at which known reserves of economically exploitable ores have been increasing. One firm, Rio Tinto Zinc, has used figures on reported reserves from 1931 to 1971 to calculate the growth-rate of 'probable reserves' of lead, zinc, and bauxite. The figures showed that reported reserves of these three minerals had been growing at 4·72 per cent, 2·82 per cent and 7·12 per cent per annum respectively—rather faster than post-war consumption in the case of lead, but slower than consumption for the other two. It does not appear to us that much can be inferred from these figures. Exploration costs money and will not be pushed beyond a certain point (perhaps when 20 years' worth of consumption at present rates has been located). The fact that known reserves of zinc and bauxite appear to be expanding more slowly than consumption may well indicate that mining companies assume— probably correctly—that the growth in consumption of these metals will be less rapid in the future. Thus the figures may tell us something about the way companies explore for minerals; but they give no indication as to trends in the real costs of discovery and extraction.

There is little systematic evidence on trends in discovery costs, but what there is does not justify unmixed optimism. Two Canadian mineral economists, Cranstone and Martin, published an interesting paper in April 1973 entitled 'Are Ore Discovery Costs Increasing?' In their paper, which covered non-ferrous metals (excluding aluminium) and uranium, they showed that the average cost of exploration 'per discovery' had risen from $2 million in 1946–50 to $14 million in 1966–70 (prices in 1971 dollars). Against this, however, had to be set the larger tonnages of contained metal discovered in the latter part of the period they were considering. When allowance was made for this, they found that exploration costs as a fraction of the value of discovered metal has doubled over the period—from $1 to $2 per $120 worth of metal. Although the authors were at pains to point out that annual exploration costs are relatively small (say 4 per cent of the value of metal production), a doubling in these costs over a 20-year period (i.e. a 3½ per cent annual rise in exploration costs) is serious enough to temper excessive optimism about cheap supplies of mineral resources in the future—especially as these data refer to an extremely resource rich country. The authors did, however, admit that the reported discoveries related, on the whole, to economic ore grades, and that several 'unsuccessful' explorations had in fact yielded information about leaner ore grades which would presumably one day be exploited; but they were unable to say how important this pessimistic bias in their finding may have been.

Price and Supply

The discussion has so far concentrated on the long-term prospects for discoveries of new mineral deposits. Information on the medium term outlook (i.e. the next 10–15 years) is more readily available. An interesting—and important—question on which this information can throw light is: given existing technology, how fast are real costs of extraction likely to rise as consumption increases? Of course, technology will not remain constant, since technical, and possibly technological, progress (as defined above) will continue to mitigate —though not necessarily to outweigh—rising costs. But some indication of likely rises in costs will at least serve to quantify the demands that will be made on technology in the future. Table 3.4 presents some estimates of the price elasticity of supply of various minerals. (A supply elasticity of 1·0 implies that, other things being equal, the price of metal must rise at the same average rate as consumption; a figure of 2·0 implies that prices need only rise half as fast as consumption.)

Table 3.4. *Elasticity of Supply of Selected Minerals, 1973*

	Price range (cents per lb)	Tonnage range (million tonnes)	Implied average supply elasticity
Aluminium	27–37	2,980–4,250	1·15
Copper	52–75	310–415	0·77
Nickel	128–200	42–90	2·03
Lead	14–20	52–93	1·84
Zinc	16–25	119–236	1·75
Uranium (U_3O_8)	7·52–69·32*	0·03–2·84	11·40

* Dollars per lb.
Source: U.S. Bureau of Mines, *Commodity Statements, 1973*.

The figures are not directly comparable since the uranium figures refer to the United States alone, whereas the estimates for the other metals include deposits in the rest of the world. However, the broad implication is clear enough. A 1 per cent rise in the uranium price will bring forth (i.e. make worth while) a 10 per cent rise in available deposits, whereas the same relative increase in copper and aluminium prices will only bring forth about 1 per cent more metal. Nickel, lead, and zinc occupy an intermediate position, with supplies increasing about one-third as fast again as price. Technical progress can probably offset the cost increases of lead and nickel, while the potential cost increase of aluminium will almost certainly be nullified by the changes in basic technology outlined above. Copper appears to present the greatest problem, as technical improvements of over 4 per cent per annum would be required to keep its cost stable. Past data indicates that, although technical progress has staved off the worst effects of declining ore grades of copper, it has not prevented the real costs (and the price) from rising. U.S. Bureau of Mines figures show that the average grade of U.S. copper ore fell by over 50 per cent (from about 1·5 per cent to 0·7 per cent) in the 40 years from 1925–65. Taking long-term movements in price as an indication of cost changes in marginal mines, it can be calculated that these costs rose by about 40 per cent (from 34 cents per lb. to 46·5 cents in 1973 values) over the same period. Clearly, technology has prevented costs from rising *pari passu* with declining ore grades; equally clearly, it has not succeeded in offsetting rising costs entirely.

Much discussion of natural resources assumes that there is a fixed inventory which is gradually being depleted. Although some natural resources are certainly being depleted, the static concept of a fixed inventory must be challenged. Not only do the relative values of different natural resources change over time: valueless rocks and minerals can also change status and become valuable natural resources as the result of changes in the technical or economic environment, either because low-cost supplies of a natural resource used for a particular purpose begin to run out or because of an exogenous technical breakthrough. This dynamic process has very little to do with sheer physical availability of resources: aluminium, the most abundant metal in the earth's crust, only began to be produced commercially in this century, because of technical difficulties in smelting it. In the case of aluminium, it may nevertheless be reasonably argued that the metal's very abundance was an important stimulus to research into ways of recovering it. The same does not, however, apply to uranium, a rather rare element which only entered the category of natural resources after the development of nuclear fission. The case of uranium is also illuminating in that only a fraction (about 1/140) of the world's natural uranium is in the form of the readily fissile isotope U-235, the remainder consisting largely of the potentially fertile but far less readily fissionable U-238. However, with the advent of fast breeder reactors, which convert U-238 into fissile isotopes of plutonium at a particularly high rate, the energy value of the world's reserves of uranium is effectively multiplied to an extent which means that even rock with a very low uranium content may become economic to mine.

What this brings out is the fact that, as E. W. Zimmermann has put it, 'Resources are not; they become'.[2] That does not mean reserves of natural resources are infinite—far from it. But it does mean that man has been, and is still, rather fickle in his choice of natural resources, being quite prepared to forsake one for another that will serve his purposes. Thus, copper, which has been mined from millennia but only truly came into its own with the widespread use of electricity, has lost much ground to aluminium in several electrical uses, despite its superior conductivity (aluminium's conductivity per unit *cost* being lower). Analogous examples from the energy sector are too well known to need repeating here.

An awareness of the fluid and ever-changing nature of natural resources is also a good antidote to a common form of myopia which leads to the following argument: since most natural resource reserves are more costly than those currently being extracted (because they are less accessible or of a lower ore grade), the real costs—in terms of labour and capital—of procuring future supplies of natural resources must rise. This is true enough in the short to medium term, simply because there is a general tendency under various economic systems, to put it no more strongly, to exploit the lowest-cost natural resources first; the necessary corollary is that those sources *not* being exploited must have higher costs under current technology. But current technology is not immutable, and changes come about both in extraction techniques and in the use of natural resources as inputs into final goods. The former tendency is a slow and steady one, while the latter only makes itself felt—usually dramatically—at discrete intervals. To see that there is no long-term tendency to use ever more expensive natural resources, it is sufficient to reflect on the historical order in which different energy sources have been used: dung, wood, peat, coal, oil, uranium.

The general conclusion of this analysis is that the key issues which will determine the future trend of the availability and cost of resources are technological. Will the technology of exploration improve rapidly enough to uncover enough new resources without undue cost increases? Will the technology of extraction move ahead fast enough to match falling ore grades? And, if either of these do not happen, will manufacturing technology offer substitution possibilities at a reasonable cost? Long-run real price trends suggest that, so far, technological and technical progress in the areas mentioned above has contained potential price rises in many minerals, and we have indicated that there are at least some concrete prospects of further advances. However, this should not lull the reader into Panglossian optimism. There may well be problems with particular minerals, and these may give rise to the need for rapid and perhaps painful adjustment in some parts of the economy. This process of structural change may itself be an inflationary factor. Our analysis has ignored these problems by concentrating on the long term and the world as a whole. Another issue of potential difficulty, with major implications, is the impact of changing resource technology upon international economic and political relationships. Technical developments and different patterns of resource extraction in the future may alter quite radically the value of the resource endowment of particular countries. The balance-of-payments effects could be substantial, and there may well be significant alterations in the balance of political power as a consequence. These problems are not insignificant; on the contrary, they will almost certainly have a far greater impact on the world we live in than will any physical shortage of minerals. But they are essentially economic and political, rather than physical, problems, exacerbated by growing shortages and rising costs of particular minerals, with ramifications which affect the entire economy, and not merely the 'mineral sector', narrowly defined. It is for this reason that we deal with them in a separate chapter.

Notes

1. S. G. Lasky, 'How Tonnage-Grade Relations Help Product Ore Reserves', *Engineering Mining Journal* 151 (4), 91–5.

2. E. W. Zimmermann, *Introduction to World Resources*, 1964.

3 The energy equation

In the previous chapter, we outlined reasons for rejecting crude theories about the physical exhaustion of resources. The situation of energy resources is rather different, however, and demands a separate treatment. Fear about the depletion of energy resources—and especially of fossil fuels—is the commonest of the fears about resource depletion. It also reflects what is, perhaps, the strongest case for pessimism about resources, even if our own conclusion is not essentially pessimistic.

Energy can be obtained by exploiting a wide variety of sources: solar radiation, moving water or air (rivers, tides, and winds), animal muscles, geothermal heat, nuclear fission and fusion, or the combustion of fuels such as wood, dung, and the 'fossil fuels' (mineral oil, coal, peat, and natural gas). The fossil fuels are, however, unique: in the degree to which energy is concentrated in them, and in the extent to which, being the product of extremely slow geological processes, they are virtually non-renewable. In economic terms, they represent accumulated capital, whereas other energy sources are more akin to income.

In one sense, all energy, once consumed, has gone beyond recall and cannot be 're-cycled'. In another sense, the value of energy expended in manufacturing, in construction, or in land improvement remains embodied in the capital equipment and infra-structure produced. A country with many years of development behind it has a large stock of energy which has thus been 'saved' by being embodied in durable equipment. More significantly for the present purpose, energy is also 'saved' through the processing of raw materials. An obsolete or broken machine may be unusable, but the recoverable materials it contains still embody the energy expended in processing them. To the extent that less energy is used in recovering and refining scrap materials than in producing the same materials from primary sources, advantage is being taken of 'saved' energy.

Even if single units are used for its statistical measurement, energy is not homogeneous; many applications require energy in a specific form. Aircraft engines, for example, require a highly concentrated source of energy to achieve an adequate power/weight ratio. Ore reduction requires fuels with a particular chemical content, burning speed, and temperature. Electrolytic processes require electricity. Even if, in some areas, energy in a specific final form might be obtained from a variety of primary sources, the cost of using any but the cheapest primary source might make the production process concerned uneconomic.

Although energy obviously plays a central rôle in economic development, it represents only a remarkably small percentage of the world's economic output. In the United States, for instance, the consumption of basic energy resources accounts for only 2·3 per cent of gross national product. In the rest of the world, it averages the even lower figure of 1·6 per cent. What makes it, nevertheless, a subject of such universal concern is that, unlike any other resource except labour, energy enters into every sector of the economy as an input which, if small, is also vital. At the same time, it follows that the key factor in the energy equation is not the cost of energy but its availability. On average, a doubling of energy cost over five years would only 'pre-empt' an extra 0·4 per cent of economic product each year —an increase which, given overall economic growth, could easily be accommodated without reducing real incomes. However, a reduction of energy availability by 50 per cent over five years would virtually paralyse large sectors of the economy and substantially change the life-style of a modern industrial society.

The Pre-eminent Case of Oil

Against this background, it becomes easier to understand why fear about the depletion of energy resources has focused so strongly upon one fossil fuel, oil (and, to a lesser extent, upon the natural gas often geologically associated with it). Oil and its products provide the forms of energy specifically required in a number of applications and provided supplies continue to be available in the future the level of prices will be relatively unimportant.

From the early 1950s to the late 1960s world energy consumption grew at nearly 5 per cent a year, closely matching the growth of domestic product and/or industrial production in most of the advanced countries. At the same time, however, the world's consumption of oil was growing by about 7·6 per cent a year. Indeed, oil and natural gas together covered nearly 80 per cent of all the incremental demand for fuels (Table 3.1).

The high compound rates at which oil and gas consumption has been growing would be less significant if reserves of these fuels were widely dispersed and abundant. In fact, they are neither. In the first place, as Table 3.2 shows, almost 70 per cent of the world's 'proved' reserves of oil and almost a third of the 'proved' reserves of gas are concentrated in the Middle East and Africa alone. In the second place, total reserves, in relation to growing rates of consumption,

Table 3.1. *World Energy Consumption, 1950-1970*
(million tonnes coal equivalent)

	1951–1955 *Average* Amount	*Percentage*	1966–1969 *Average* Amount	*Percentage*
Coal, Peat, etc.	1,669·4	56·3	2,276·3	38·6
Oil	802·0	27·0	2,327·7	39·5
Natural Gas	359·6	12·1	1,149·3	19·5
Other*	135·4	4·6	139·4	2·4
Total	2,966·4	100·0	5,892·7	100·0

* Hydroelectric and nuclear.

Source: The Wharton School, University of Pennsylvania, *Materials Requirements in the United States and Abroad in the Year 2000*, Washington, D.C., 1973.

Table 3.2. *World's 'Proved' Oil and Natural Gas Reserves, 1973*

	Oil Reserves millions of tonnes	% share	Gas Reserves millions of tonnes oil equivalent	% share
Western Europe	2,115·0	2·5	4,735·0	9·4
Caribbean, South America	4,303·0	5·0	2,252·0	4·5
Middle East	47,622·0	55·8	10,193·0	20·4
Africa	9,153·0	10·7	4,629·0	9·2
Indonesia	1,428·0	1·7	370·4	0·7
Other Asia	355·0	0·4	1,147·0	2·3
Australia, New Zealand	343·0	0·4	1,300·0	2·6
North America	6,001·0	7·0	7,339·0	14·6
U.S.S.R.	10,880·0	12·8	17,410·0	34·8
China	2,720·0	3·2	493·0	1·0
Other Communist	408·0	0·5	232·0	0·5
World	85,388·0	100·0	50,144·0	100·0

Source: Oil and Gas Journal, 31st December, 1973.

Table 3.3. *Oil Supply and Demand Position, 1973*

Oil Reserves (billion tonnes)	Consumption (billion tonnes)	Years' supply at various rates of annual growth in demand				
		4%	5%	6%	7%	8%
January 1973	*1973*					
'Proved' 86·0	2·77	20	19	18	17	16
'Possible' 220*	2·77	36	32	30	28	26

* Geologically possible and recoverable with known techniques, including proved reserves (BP estimate).
Source: BP, Commodity Research Unit, and industry estimates.

are far from abundant (Table 3.3). 'Proved' reserves of oil—those recoverable with current techniques at a currently economic cost—would be exhausted by the late 1980s if consumption were to continue to grow at 7·6 per cent a year, and even the much larger volume of 'possible' reserves would, in those circumstances, be used up by about the year 2000. In practice, of course, supply would start to tail off long before those dates; indeed, it seems doubtful that an annual growth of 7·6 per cent could be sustained even until 1980.

At first sight this situation arouses not only alarm but also amazement. The world's rush to use oil—to build its industries and base its habits of life upon a dwindling resource—looks astonishingly short-sighted. How could so many countries have permitted themselves to become dependent upon a commodity likely to be used up within a lifetime? Would it not have been better to have based continued development upon, say, coal, of which there are ample world reserves (Table 3.4)? The simple answer is that so far oil has been freely available and has enjoyed cost advantages. Economics is concerned with choices between better and worse materials or between methods of work involving cheaper or dearer inputs, and oil-using methods have hitherto, on the whole, been both particularly convenient and relatively cheap.

During the later 1960s, the cheapness of oil was obvious enough, as its real price declined. Even in the two years before October 1973, price rises little more than made up for that decline. Since October 1973, however, oil has ceased to seem so cheap, even if it remains competitive with a range of other energy sources. In theory, that change should have helped to bring home the potential shortage of oil and to encourage precautionary action. The first signal of growing scarcity in a market economy is a rise in price; when the rise is sufficient, users are obliged either to reduce consumption or to switch to more abundant, and thus cheaper, substitutes. In practice, the very fact that energy costs constitute such a small proportion of average final production costs makes it more difficult for the price mechanism to work effectively in promoting such an adjustment to a scarcity of oil. In such circumstances, when the commodity in short supply has relatively little effect on final prices, cost increases can more easily be passed on to customers or absorbed in other ways. Price effects alone may then not result in a rapid enough reaction to the growing shortage, and the crisis may be sharpened by being delayed.

Even if the need to reduce oil consumption and to develop alternatives were well enough recognized (as it probably now is), the fact that energy represents only a small part of final industrial costs would hinder the normal operation of the price mechanism in another respect. Neither industrial users nor energy suppliers can change to alternative sources of energy without spending time and money. Industry will do so when the relative price difference between a current source of energy and its alternative is enough to promise an equivalent saving in total costs in the immediate future. Energy suppliers will do so when an adequate demand for alternatives can be expected to develop sufficiently quickly. One theoretical rôle of the

Table 3.4. *World Proven Solid Fuel Reserves, 1968*
(million tonnes oil equivalent)

Country	Proven*	Inferred*	Total	Percentage share
Western Europe	32,350	44,350	76,700	1·3
Poland	26,000	14,800	40,800	0·7
U.S.S.R. (including Asian U.S.S.R.)	166,000	3,575,000	3,741,000	63·6
South Africa	24,500	24,500	49,000	0·8
Other Africa	4,000	5,570	9,750	0·2
China	—	680,000	680,000	11·6
India	8,500	64,750	73,250	1·2
Other Asia	6,500	15,750	22,250	0·4
North America	95,000	990,000	1,085,000	18·5
Central and S. America	2,500	21,950	24,450	0·4
Australasia	35,500	40,500	76,000	1·3
World Total	400,850	5,477,350	5,878,200	100·0

* These terms differ from the oil industry's 'Proved' and 'Possible'. 'Proven' coal deposits at workable depths and in seams of reasonable thickness can be accurately measured but are not necessarily wholly recoverable. 'Inferred' deposits are those of a similar depth and seam thickness which geologists expect to find in place in view of the size and distributory of 'Proven' deposits.
Source: Commodities Research Unit and National Coal Board estimates.

price mechanism is thus to make the development of alternatives profitable at a rate which ensures that they will reach the market in good time to off-set scarcity. In the case of energy resources, however, the price difference between current and alternative forms will have to be very large in order to have that effect, simply because energy itself is such a small element in total costs.

All these considerations make the oil situation somewhat different from that of the metals described in Chapter 2. It was argued there that, under the stimulus of rising real prices, a combination of substitution and improvements in the technology of resource discovery and extraction could avert a 'resource crisis', in the sense of a sudden curtailment of supply. Those options apply to the oil situation as well. In the first place, however, the price mechanism, as we have seen, is hampered in its application to oil. In the second place, known reserves of oil represent fewer years of expected consumption than for any other major resource. In the third place, because of the heavy concentration of oil reserves in the Middle East, the oil situation is peculiarly vulnerable to a sudden curtailment of supply on non-economic grounds. What makes oil—and thus energy—a source of particular concern is not that theoretical possibilities of off-setting resource scarcity are lacking in this case but that, for all these reasons, there is so much doubt as to whether they can be exploited swiftly enough in practice to match the pace at which oil supply may itself be constrained.

The fact remains that, because of the current and future oil situation, there will have to be an adjustment during the next few years from cheap and plentiful energy to dearer and scarcer energy. In the longer term, that means developing alternatives to 'conventional' mineral oil. In the shorter term, however, it means limiting consumption itself, in order to ease the tensions in a period of adjustment. First, therefore, we need to consider the prospects for economy in consumption and their possible effects. Thereafter, the question of alternatives has to be examined.

Economies in a World with Less Oil

Adjustment to a scarcity of oil means much more than a simple reversion to past techniques which use energy in smaller quantities or different forms. In the first place, the fact that oil consumption has grown during a period of rapid industrialization, itself based on cheap energy, means that adjustment must now involve a much larger industrial base. In the second place, the fact that the same period has seen a rapid rise of living standards indicates that a crude resurrection of the historical past would entail a sharp decline in income levels. Nor would a return to the past automatically mean a less profligate use of energy. Our ancestors were in many cases more wasteful of resources, including energy resources, than we are ourselves. In fact, of course, advanced countries deprived of oil would not return immediately to their historical, pre-oil condition, if only because they would retain the skills which they had acquired and the capital, including 'saved' energy, which they had accumulated during the age of oil. Nevertheless, demand not only for services but also for basic materials sets some minimum level of energy consumption below which a modern industrial economy could not function as such. A drastic reduction of energy supply caused by a 'Malthusian' oil crisis would undoubtedly depress incomes and living standards. Within wide limits, however, modern economies are highly adaptable. As recently as 1950, the world managed with less than half the energy it consumed in 1973, when oil still accounted for less than half the energy supply. With that in mind, there is no obvious reason why even a 'Malthusian' oil crisis should cause social collapse.

There are, in fact, no grounds for expecting such a severe crisis, but there are good reasons for seeking the sort of economies which can eke out 'conventional' oil supplies in the shorter term, while alternative energy sources are developed for the longer term. Provided these can be found, the question of an economic upheaval, with a return to techniques of 25, or even 10, years ago need not arise.

Many possibilities exist for economizing through the substitution of other fuels for oil. In some economic sectors, however, certain fuels are technically essential. In particular, because motor vehicles

Table 3.5. *Annual Energy and Oil Consumption by User Sector, Western Industrialized Countries 1972*

Sector	Oil (million tonnes)	Oil percentage of consumption met by oil	Total Energy million tonnes oil equivalent	Oil: % of Total
Domestic and Commercial	440	58·2	755	25·3
Industrial	400	36·9	1,070	23·0
Transport	620	96·7	635	35·6
Electricity generation	280	40·3	695	16·1
Total	1,740	55·1	3,155	100·0

Source: BP and Commodity Research Unit and industry estimates.

and aircraft have to use oil-based fuels, the transport sector is one in which it is almost impossible, in the short run, to substitute out of oil. In contrast, almost any energy source can be used in electricity generation, so that, even in the short run, the substitution potential in that sector is particularly high. The starting point for any consideration of economies is therefore the estimates of current distribution of oil consumption between different economic sectors in the Western industrial countries (Table 3.5). Possible energy savings can then be considered within each sector in turn.

Domestic and Commercial Sector. In this first sector, which draws 58 per cent of its energy from oil, the major use of energy is for space heating, and a great deal of that energy is wasted simply through the poor insulation of buildings. Some economies are certainly available here, even if the potential for savings varies widely between countries, because of differences in climate or existing insulation standards. Additional savings could be achieved by the increased use of district heating techniques, which can take advantage of economies of scale, of fuels unsuitable for individual home heating or of waste heat from power stations. Another possibility is simply to reduce heating standards; recent estimates suggest that a reduction of only 3 degrees Fahrenheit in all American houses, offices and shops would save 12 per cent of the fuel oil and 14 per cent of the natural gas consumed in a typical winter.

It would be wrong to overestimate the scale of the economies available in this sector. Figures produced by the European Commission in October 1972 implied that a reduction of even 15 per cent in the expected consumption of energy in 1985 for domestic space heating and cooking in the six original member countries of the European Community would save the equivalent of only some 29 million tons of oil in that year, which represents less than two years' growth of demand in the domestic sector alone.[1] Such savings would not, therefore, postpone for long the depletion of energy resources. At the same time, readily available economies in the domestic sector, which could certainly bear without undue discomfort a consumption cut of 10, or even 20, per cent, could help to ease demand in a period of transition to alternative sources of energy.

Transport Sector. Transport, in the industrial Western countries, draws more than 96 per cent of its energy from oil. The transport sector must thus be that most heavily affected by any short-term oil supply crisis. At the same time, the wide distribution of interdependent industries within and between countries, together with the extent to which many people's lives are organized around the existence of relatively inexpensive public and private passenger transport, means that it must be difficult to achieve economies in the short run simply by using less transport. More realistic opportunities for saving exist, however, through switching to (or retaining) forms of transport which are less extravagant of energy: small cars and motorcycles instead of larger ones; rail and bus or coach transport instead of private motoring; the postponement of energy-intensive vehicle programmes such as the Advanced Passenger Train or the supersonic air transport; the fuller exploitation of economies of scale in conventional sea and air transport.

Quantitatively, the most important savings are likely to be available in the field of motor transport. The internal combustion engine is a remarkably inefficient means of converting the energy of oil into motive power: the best petrol engines achieve conversion rates of only 14–18 per cent, and even diesel engines convert only about 21 per cent of fuel energy into motive power. Even if it would be premature to consider radical alternatives, such as the direct-burning fuel cells which could have theoretical conversion rates of 50–70 per cent, considerable savings could be obtained merely by switching to less extravagant motor cars of existing design; the most economical cars in use already consume 35–40 per cent less fuel than the average. Further economy could come from banning private motoring in city centres, which is fuel-intensive and where alternative public transport is easiest to organize. A 50 per cent cut in energy consumption for private motoring alone in Western Europe, Japan, and North America might save about 82 million tonnes of oil a year by 1985. Once again, this is not a spectacular economy, but it might represent the right degree of saving at the right time during a relatively short crisis of adjustment.

One point to be noted is that, in the transport field, techniques designed to eliminate pollution tend also to increase fuel consumption. Legislation to restrict aircraft noise or to set emission standards for motor vehicles is likely to be costly in terms of fuel, and such environmental protection measures might have to be modified or postponed during a fuel scarcity.

Industrial Sector. Western industry, which derives about 37 per cent of its energy from oil, has a constant incentive to increase fuel efficiency, as part of the ordinary effort to cut costs of all kinds. Improving the insulating properties of furnace refractory bricks reduces fuel consumption per unit of steel output. Evolution of the pyro-technology of copper smelting yields small annual savings. Developments in the electrolytic smelting of aluminium devised by Alcoa will, it is reported, mean a 20 per cent reduction in energy consumption. Much larger savings might result, however, from the sort of fundamental changes in production technique which could be provoked by a radical change in the energy supply position. It might then be worth while to change from pyro-technology to hydro-technology in the copper industry, reducing energy consumption by about one third, or to switch to the Toth (manganese-chlorine) process of aluminium production, which does not depend upon electrolysis at all.

The association in the public mind between an 'energy crisis' and the risk of environmental pollution has helped to popularize the idea of achieving fuel economy through the recycling of industrial materials. However, there is no automatic harmony of energy-saving and environmental protection policies. As a source of lower grade pulp, recycled paper, for example, can both save energy and reduce the dumping of waste, but its use in higher grade paper production entails a great deal of de-inking, which produces more pollution than the processing of primary pulp. Nevertheless, reclamation of scrap metals does consume less energy and create less pollution than primary metal production, while also yielding perfect substitutes for a great many applications. At the same time, the degree of saving offered by recycling depends upon the relationship between the rate of scrap arisings and the rate at which consumption is growing. Because aluminium consumption is rising so rapidly, scrap can cover only a small proportion of production needs. On the other hand, old copper scrap could cover up to a third of demand in advanced countries, and iron and steel scrap some 30 per cent.

Although process energy waste in industry is probably much less than the waste through poor insulation in the domestic and commercial sector, it certainly exists. During the British energy crisis in the winter of 1973/74, the National Institute of Economic and Social Research estimated that a 10 per cent cut in total energy supply to industry would mean only a 6 per cent cut in total output. As that indicates, there is scope for saving at least some energy without any significant effect on production.

Electricity Generation Sector. Although this sector is only 40 per cent dependent on oil, it offers significant possibilities of substitution. One possibility is to accelerate nuclear power programmes. Because of the lead times involved and the problems of safety and waste disposal which remain, this would have only a limited effect in the shorter term: a crash programme in the Western industrial countries might save 75 million tonnes of oil in 1980 and 200 million tonnes in 1985. In the longer term, nuclear power could be one of the major factors in the equation. Meanwhile, a second possibility is a partial return to coal: by arresting the decline of coal as an electricity generating fuel, or by substituting coal for electricity in certain applications, such as heating. Some 65 per cent of original fuel energy is lost in generating and transmitting electricity. Direct use of fuel, in certain cases, could reduce the effect of that loss. Because of the time needed to develop new deposits, the short-term savings obtainable by switching to coal are obviously limited. Nevertheless, a crash programme of coal substitution might save about 180 million tonnes of oil in North America and about 220 million tonnes in Western Europe and Japan in 1985.

Building coal or nuclear power stations is not the only way to save oil in electricity generation. Generating companies have to maintain substantial spare capacity in order to meet peak demand at particular times of day. Hitherto, hydro-electric, nuclear, and oil-fired stations have carried the base load, with older coal-fired stations being brought in to meet this peak demand. By transferring the latter to the base load category and concentrating the use of oil-fired stations in peak periods, an immediate saving of oil could be achieved, on a scale which, for the United States alone, the U.S. Federal Power Commission has estimated as 16 million tonnes a year.

The measures outlined above are ones which could reduce energy and/or oil consumption without interfering with industrial production or disrupting life styles in advanced industrial societies. Their overall impact is difficult to quantify precisely, but our own estimates of the savings thus obtainable are as follows:

Domestic and commercial sector	15–20%
Transport sector	5–10%
Industrial sector	0–5%
Electricity generation sector	5%

Given the relative importance of each sector, these savings would amount to 6–10 per cent of all energy, or 10–15 per cent of oil consumption if the savings were concentrated on that fuel alone, with the economies all being achieved by 1980. Recent trends imply an 80 per cent greater oil demand in 1980 than in 1972; with these economies, we would expect it to be only 53–62 per cent greater. Such a reduction in the annual growth rate of oil consumption— from 7·6 per cent to 5·5–6·2 per cent—could significantly ease transitional problems. Allowing for these 'painless' economies, the oil consumption of the non-Communist world, which was 2,200 million tonnes in 1972, might rise by 1,150–1,350 million tonnes to a total of 3,350–3,550 million tonnes in 1980.

Energy Supply in the Longer Term

Leaving aside the issue of a political interruption of oil supplies, the economies outlined above can only lengthen the life of 'proved' and 'possible' oil reserves by a few years. Ultimately, new sources of oil and other energy will be needed. Can these be made available in adequate quantities? Will the effort needed to obtain them be so costly that other sectors of the world economy will be forced to reduce real levels of income and activity? Can the transition be made in the two decades left before oil production from existing sources begins to run out?

Some estimates can be made of the possible increase in oil supply from existing sources up to 1980, but these are of doubtful utility when some of the major producing and exporting countries are unable to spend their potential oil revenues, and thus have a reduced incentive to earn them. Libya, Kuwait, Qatar, Abu Dhabi, and Saudi Arabia are all in this category. Together, they account for about 40 per cent of non-Communist world production and for a far higher proportion of reserves. In various ways, they have all begun to question whether continued rapid expansion of production is in their best interest. Libya, Kuwait, and Qatar are anxious not to exhaust their limited reserves before developing alternative bases for their economies. Abu Dhabi and Saudi Arabia are less concerned with depletion of reserves than with the relationship between the future value of saved income from exported oil and that of oil retained in the ground. Especially in a period of unstable exchange rates, unexploited oil reserves may increase in value faster than money earning interest in a bank. Meanwhile, foreign investment is seen as risky and investment opportunities at home as narrowly limited. To increase oil production, and thus revenue, is not obviously advantageous in such circumstances. And if production is increased, the impossibility of spending more than a small part of the consequential revenue will mean that, by 1980, there will be an unprecedentedly large accumulation of liquidity in the hands of a small number of potentially unstable governments.

Other oil-producing countries, hungry for funds to support their continued development and conscious of the long-term threat from alternative fuels, can be expected to push ahead with the exploitation of their oil reserves. In the non-Communist world, the United States, Canada, Iran, Algeria, Indonesia, Norway, and the United Kingdom are all in this category, as are other countries in Western Europe, the Caribbean, Latin America, and South-East Asia whose reserves are smaller. Supply from those sources could perhaps grow at 7·5–8 per cent a year up to 1980, as against the 6·5 per cent rate of recent years. Some experts, however, would regard that as an over-optimistic expectation. For technical reasons, the optimum rate of extraction from a particular oil field is usually about 10 per cent a year of recoverable reserves; higher rates produce uneven underground 'migration' of oil and reduce the ultimately recoverable reserves, while lower rates mean higher average unit costs. An annual production increase of 7·5–8 per cent would rapidly undermine the ratio of 'proved' reserves to output in those countries which can be regarded as 'secure' sources because of their strong economic incentive to extract oil. At the same time, 'possible' (but not 'proved') reserves outside the Middle East amount to some 120–125 billion tonnes. Achieving a high production growth rate in 'secure' areas will thus depend upon the speed at which new reservoirs can be 'proved' and brought into production. On the assumption that high oil prices and government policies stimulate exploration, however, some 55–60 per cent of the oil supply needed in the shorter term can be regarded as 'secure'.

Countries whose output can be regarded as 'secure' produced about 1,320 million tonnes of oil in 1972 and might produce 2,350–2,440 million tonnes in 1980: an increase of 1,030–1,120 million tonnes. That increase is 120–230 million tonnes less than the growth needed, even allowing for the economies suggested earlier, and more than 600 million tonnes short of the demand growth implied by recent trends. Unless the 'insecure' countries also increase production, therefore, there will be a substantial 'oil gap' by 1980, even if all the readily available savings are made in consumption. That 'gap' will obviously widen if the 'insecure' suppliers, facing a growing surplus of unspendable revenue, actually reduce their production. The central question of the energy equation is whether that potential 'gap' can be bridged, by extracting oil from 'unconventional' sources or by developing other energy forms—coal, natural gas, or nuclear power—more rapidly. The alternative is for world prosperity in 1980 to depend upon the goodwill of a handful of small and under-populated countries.

Unconventional Oil Sources. Alternative sources of petroleum would involve the least adaptation cost on the part of oil users. In terms of energy content, known deposits of tar sands in Canada and Vene-zuela are more than twice as extensive as known reserves of crude oil in the Middle East. There are in addition large known deposits of shale oil in the U.S.A. and proving of unconventional sources else-where has only just begun. Production costs, from tar or shale to petroleum, are still comparatively high, and the process needs far more labour than crude oil but the technology is known and proved, and existing plants have already passed beyond the experimental pilot stage. One disadvantage is the tonnage of waste sand and gravel discarded in mining and refining, but this need be no more of a problem than is already the case in open-cast mining operations. A more serious problem is the need for great quantities of process water.

In the short term the main problem would be lead times. Known plans indicate a 1980 production from these sources of only 18·6 million tonnes oil and a 1985 figure of 52·9 million. An emergency programme might raise these figures to 25 million and 90 million tonnes respectively.

Although these unconventional sources can only make a small contribution to energy demand over the next ten years, they do ensure the ultimate availability of oil in applications, such as trans-port, where there is no substitute. There can be no question of physically running out of oil at least within the next century.

Coal. Coal remains in direct competition with oil, directly in the generation of electricity and the provision of heat for industrial pro-cesses and indirectly as a source of gas competing with natural gas and petroleum gas. Even if no more deposits of coal are discovered, supplies are adequate and well able to meet the world's likely total energy demand for many years ahead. Coal mining is more expen-sive than pumping oil, but a higher proportion of coal in the ground can be considered exploitable than is the case with oil. About 50 per cent of deposits are regarded as potentially available for use, and technical developments could improve on this. In particular, tech-niques for gasifying coal in the ground could make a number of physically or commercially unworkable mines yield some of their content.

Anti-pollution regulations and the needs of metal smelters have concentrated new coal demand on low-sulphur coal. Indeed, the full extent of oil saving from coal substitution may be possible only when a substitute for coking coal in blast furnaces is available; in the immediate future, there will continue to be a more acute shortage of low-sulphur coking coal than of oil. In the short term, oil may even have to substitute for some coal in this particular market; before the recent oil crisis, the use of oil in blast furnaces was one of the factors expected to reduce the consumption of furnace coke per tonne of cast iron produced in the European Community from 582 kg in 1970 to about 510 kg in 1975.

The shortage of coking coal is partly due to the inland transport cost of coal. Deposits of low-sulphur coal exist in the United States and possibly in Siberia, where they are easily mined but far distant from markets. Currently, where there is no access to waterways, coal transport is cheapest on unit trains, but even these are expensive in ton/mile terms. Within the next fifteen years, the technology of slurry pipelines is expected to be perfected; this could cut transport costs by 20–50 per cent, and bring the output from remote coal seams into world markets.

The only realistic possibility for a major expansion of coal production in the non-Communist world by 1980 seems to lie in open-cast mining in North America. Open-cast operations now account for about half of United States coal production and have been expanding at twice the average rate for the industry as a whole. Known reserves of 'strippable' coal amount to 45,000 million short tons (about 27,000 tonnes of oil equivalent), which is enough to last until 2015 at an annual production growth rate of 6 per cent (more than sufficient for any transition period). Additional 'strippable' reserves are believed to contain another 73,000 million short tons (about 44,000 million tonnes of oil equivalent). The U.S. National Petroleum Council has made estimates based upon doubling open-cast production of coal by 1985, while also increasing underground production by some 30 per cent. On that basis, United States exports of coal as a fuel might reach the equivalent of 245 million tonnes of oil in 1980, rising to 360 million tonnes in 1985.

Natural Gas. Natural gas is clean, has high thermal efficiency and can be produced, in most cases, at relatively low cost. In countries with established gas distribution structures, it will continue for many years to meet a significant proportion of energy demand, even when domestic gasfields are depleted and supply continues from imports. At the same time, reserves of natural gas, which are often associated with oil reserves, are similarly limited. Given that limitation and the long lead time and heavy investment involved in constructing new distribution networks, it cannot be expected that natural gas will do much to bridge the potential 'oil gap' by 1980.

Nuclear Power. Although nuclear power stations already contribute substantially to energy supply in a number of countries, nuclear energy has consistently disappointed predictions. The time needed for development in a new field of technology has regularly been under-estimated. The temperatures and pressures generated within reactors and radiation itself have caused unanticipated structural damage, and many reactors have thus been forced to operate below designed output levels.

Nuclear fuels are difficult to handle, and the products of their fission, including plutonium, are highly toxic and potentially dangerous. On the other hand, the raw materials for nuclear fuel—uranium and thorium—are relatively plentiful and, in relation to their energy content, cheap to produce. Because the readily fissionable isotope of uranium (U-235) forms only about 0·7 per cent of the naturally-occurring material, current reactors can exploit only a small proportion of the energy theoretically available. Techniques for recycling plutonium, which is derived from the abundant U-238 isotope, are, however, being developed. Thereafter, the fast breeder reactor (FBR), by using plutonium as well as uranium as a fuel and by converting a substantial proportion of the U-238 to plutonium, will not only be able to extract the maximum energy value from its own fuel but will also produce somewhat more fissile material than it consumes.

If the remaining problems of FBR design can be solved, the availability of raw materials for nuclear fuels will cease to be an important resource constraint. If, at an unpredictably further remove, the enormous difficulty of generating electricity from nuclear fusion, rather than fission, can be resolved, resources for producing energy in that form can be regarded as effectively limitless. All of this, however, lies far beyond 1980. Meanwhile, even when the technical problems of existing thermal reactors are overcome, nuclear energy is likely to make only a small contribution to bridging the potential 'oil gap'. Ultimately, it has the potential to guarantee adequate electricity supply indefinitely, but the nuclear industry has had many false dawns, and 'ultimately' may be further away than is often supposed.

The Energy Equation in 1980

Table 3.6 summarizes what has been said about the oil situation up to 1980, which appears to be a critical year beyond which—but only beyond which—new sources of energy can begin to have a major effect. One thing which is clear from this table is that, unless the 'surplus' oil producers (Libya, Kuwait, Qatar, Abu Dhabi, and Saudi Arabia included) actually reduce production, non-disruptive consumption economies combined with the maximum feasible expansion of oil supplies from outside the 'surplus' countries, the marginal development of 'unconventional' oil and a crash coal programme, will be just about enough to match supply to demand. Without the consumption economies, sufficiency will depend upon the 'surplus' countries expanding their production at a substantial rate. In any case, the situation will be tight enough to mean that both energy suppliers and workers in energy industries will be in a strong market position. Energy, in short, will be a sellers' market during the rest of the 1970s, in contrast to the buyers' market which prevailed in the 1960s.

Table 3.6. *The Oil Equation in 1980 (Non-communist world)*
(million tonnes oil equivalent)

Oil Supply	1972	1980
Surplus countries*	880	880
Other countries	1,320	2,350 to 2,440
Shale oil, syncrude, etc.	—	25
Crash coal programme	—	90
Total	2,200	3,345 to 3,435
Oil Demand		
At trend rate	2,200	3,960
As above, with consumption economies	2,200	3,350 to 3,550
Balance		
Without economies	—	−525 to −610
With economies	—	−5 to −115
Required growth of oil supply		
from surplus countries (% p.a.)		
Without economies	—	6·0 to 6·8
With economies	—	nil to 1·5

* Libya, Kuwait, Qatar, Abu Dhabi, Saudi Arabia.
Source: Commodities Research Unit and industry estimates.

Long-Term Energy Prices

It appears from the earlier discussion that, even if the growth rate of consumption is reduced, 'unconventional' energy sources will have to be developed to cater for demand by 1980. These unconventional sources are higher cost than current sources, and it follows that energy prices will have to rise in order to justify investment in them.

In the longer term, as we have seen, consumption can be restrained and substitutions made. Indeed, these are probable responses to rising prices; there is no evidence to suggest that demand is price inelastic in the long term. This means that the market price will return to a point where the price equals marginal production costs. These marginal costs will, however, be those of 'unconventional' oil sources, which will be considerably higher than those prevailing before October 1973.

Table 3.7 gives some estimates of the possible market price of various energy resources in 1980 on this basis, compared with 1973 pre-crisis forecasts. The figures refer to constant money values; in other words, the increases are additional to any general inflation of prices.

It is worth making a number of comments on these forecasts. Firstly, the 1980 prices suggested are in many cases below current prices. In other words, the rise in prices that took place in the winter of 1973–4 was sufficient to justify the exploitation of most 'unconventional' sources. Secondly, the 1980 prices for coal and gas reflect not the production costs of coal, but the production costs of oil plus (in the case of gas) or minus (in the case of coal) a premium. This weighting reflects the differences of equality, ease of handling and convenience between the various fuels. Thirdly, it must be appreciated that the price of all petroleum products will probably not increase at the same rate as the price of a barrel of crude oil. The prices of different petroleum products will increase at different rates. The 'heavy' oils compete directly with coal and low BTU gas from coal, and their prices will be held down by this. Refiners will maximize output of middle and higher distillates like jet fuel and gasoline and concentrate price rises on these.

Finally, the prices given in Table 3.7 relate to production costs for the unconventional sources based on existing technology. It is reasonable to expect that some progress will be made in improving extraction methods, so that the actual increase will be less, but, even taking an extremely pessimistic view, the world, in the long term, is certainly not going to have to devote more than three times as many

Table 3.7. *Energy Price Forecasts, 1980*
(*per barrel of oil equivalent in 1973$*)

North America delivered East Coast	1973 pre crisis average	1980 'under-lying' cost	per cent increase	price limit based on marginal costs	possible upper limit to prices
Oil	5·00	7·10	42·0	4·30	11·50
Coal	2·45	4·40	79·6	2·45	6·30
Manufactured gas:					
Low BTU	n.a.	6·50	140·7*	3·60	9·00
High BTU	n.a.	9·80	263·0*	6·00	14·00
Natural gas	2·70	8·10	200	6·00	14·00
Western Europe landed					
Oil	5·40	9·70	79·6	5·60	15·00
Coal: Indigenous	3·80	4·75	25·0	3·50	8·20
Imported	3·05	3·80	24·6	2·60	8·20
Manufactured gas:					
Low BTU	n.a.	8·25*	83·3	4·75	9·40
High BTU	n.a.	11·20*	148·9	7·60	18·00
Natural gas	4·50	11·20	148·9	7·60	18·00
Japan landed					
Oil	5·20	10·25	97·0	6·80	15·00
Coal	3·00	5·90	96·1	3·90	8·20
Manufactured gas:					
Low BTU	n.a.	7·95	62·2*	4·75	9·40
High BTU	n.a.	10·70	118·4*	7·15	15·50
Natural gas	4·90	10·70	118·4	7·15	15·50

* Increase on natural gas price.
Source: Commodities Research Unit and industry estimates.

resources, in terms of labour and capital, to oil extraction as it does at present. At present, some 2 per cent of world resources are devoted to the energy industry, but only about 1·5 per cent is specifically devoted to oil and gas. This might have to increase to 4·5 per cent of the total, giving an overall 5 per cent of world output devoted energy. Thus, the cost of compensating for the impending scarcity of certain energy resources represents less than 3 per cent of one year's output, equivalent to one year's growth at current rates. Moreover, this change to new oil and energy sources is likely to spread over at least a decade, so that the annual effect on the world economy will be scarcely noticeable. Indeed, the recent crisis may prove to be the worst of the shocks involved. Provided that any sudden reduction in oil supplies for non-economic reasons can be avoided, and provided that steps are taken promptly to achieve modest consumption economies, to promote substitution and to develop new oil and energy sources, there is no reason why the energy equation should not balance in the medium and long term. Those provisos, however, are clearly laden with political implications, internationally and domestically.

Note

1. Commission of the European Communities, *Prospects of Primary Energy Demand in the Community* (*1975–1980–1985*), SEC (72) 3283 Final, Brussels, 4 October 1972.

4 An economic overview

In the preceding chapters we have examined the nature of mineral resources and have suggested certain provisional conclusions about resource scarcity: first, that metal ores are still very abundant, although a slow upward trend in costs of extraction is possible unless progress in extractive technology can keep pace with declining ore grades, and second, that a sudden disruption of oil supplies could have a serious impact on industrialized countries, although, in the longer run, alternative fuels could fill the gap at the cost of some considerable increase in price. We must next ask what effects these factors will have on international trade and on national economies.

As far as international trade is concerned, a rise in the price of raw materials must initially increase the export earnings of those selling the raw materials and raise the import costs of those who buy them. Importing countries will have to devote more resources to making up for these higher costs through exporting more of their own goods and services, while those selling raw materials will be able to buy those goods and services without in turn having to export more. In other words, the immediate effect will be to redistribute income from the consumers of raw materials to producers through the mechanism of the terms of trade. Later, however, those with declining relative incomes will try to protect themselves by reducing their consumption of raw materials or by substitution from dear materials to those that are more plentiful and cheap. This will reduce the growth in the demand for the former and cause prices to level off and fall. Thus, from the consumers' point of view, the adverse movement in the terms of trade will be arrested. Only if there is general resource scarcity will this not necessarily happen—and one of the main conclusions we have already drawn is that there is little likelihood of general resource scarcity in the foreseeable future.

There are additional grounds for believing that an initial shift in the terms of trade in favour of those who produce raw materials and against those who consume them will not be sustained. Over the past 30 years the terms of trade have moved steadily against raw material producers, except for disturbances such as the Korean War boom and the present (1974) situation. The fundamental reason for this is that technical and technological progress has economized in the use of raw materials per unit of output. Advances in metallurgy have produced alloys which are cheaper than the metals previously used. Fuel economy has increased. Although modern society may seem profligate in its consumption of goods, it is less so in terms of the raw materials needed to make them. In addition, technical progress causes labour costs to rise in real terms relative to those of raw materials and capital. Since manufactured goods and services contain a much higher labour content than raw materials, this trend helps to raise production costs of the former relative to the latter, and this movement is eventually reflected in relative prices.

Economists concerned with the problems of the primary producing developing countries, such as Raoul Prebisch,[1] have long argued that there is actually a chronic tendency for the terms of trade to move against these countries. That has been the main justification for advocating a policy of industrial development behind protective tariff, quota, and non-tariff barriers for the developing countries. The prices of raw materials have been said, in particular, to be limited by the possibility of producing substitutes in advanced countries. Increased production serves to drive down prices, while reduced production serves only to provoke this substitution. On the other hand, developing countries are said to be unable, owing to their weak market power, to influence the price of the manufactured and service imports they have to make. They are thus 'price takers' as regards both exports and imports.

It is not our purpose to analyse the Prebisch thesis and its variants. Attention is drawn to it merely in order to point out that we have no real evidence that its fundamental tenets will cease to apply in the future. The so-called resource crisis will have very little long-term effect on the balance of power between economies because it is only a temporary phenomenon. Even the limitation on oil availability, which presents the most serious resource problem, need cause only temporary difficulties for energy production and consumption. However, there are, in addition, balance of payments effects and resource cost effects of the oil problem. The magnitudes of these, and the manner in which they may affect economies in the long term, need to be examined in more detail.

The close association between economic growth and energy demand—satisfied at the margin by oil in almost all countries—makes it relatively simple to calculate the extra oil required for any given increase in GDP and to adjust this for whatever price rises are thought likely to occur, thus arriving at an estimate of the extra balance of payments cost of higher oil prices. Such an estimate has been made in Table 4.1 for the fifteen major Western consuming countries, which together account for 67 per cent of oil demand. For this purpose, an oil price of $8·50 per barrel f.o.b. has been assumed. In addition, due allowance has been made for a slowdown in industrial production and GDP following the oil supply crisis in the winter of 1973/74.

Table 4.1. *Additional Costs of Oil Imports, 1974*

Country	Estimates of extra oil cost $mn
Canada	−1,750 (net benefit)
United States	15,000
Japan	11,200
Austria	370
Belgium	1,500
Denmark	750
France	4,700
Germany	5,000
Italy	4,100
Netherlands	1,400
Norway	350
Spain	1,500
Sweden	1,200
Switzerland	500
United Kingdom	4,500
Total	50,320

Assumptions: Oil price of $8·50 per barrel f.o.b. (i.e. $10·50–11·00 c.i.f. Europe).
Source: Commodities Research Unit estimates.

The question to be raised in the context of Table 4.1 is whether, if these countries restrict demand by deflation to meet their extra balance of payments cost in 1974 of about $50,000 mn, this could lead to a world recession.

The additional balance of payments deficit of the oil-importing countries will become the oil-exporting states' increased surplus. The precise size of the surplus depends on oil prices, taxing policies and rates of exploitation. For the exporting states with small populations

—Saudi Arabia, Libya, Kuwait, and Abu Dhabi—estimates of the annual surplus by 1982 range upwards from $60,000 mn. These funds could be invested in industrial countries, providing a capital inflow to balance the current account deficit, and making deflation unnecessary. By financing investment in this way, domestic savings ratios could fall and consumption be maintained. The effect on growth rates would be indeterminate. Alternatively, the surplus funds could accumulate in liquid form. Used to speculate on currency markets, the funds could cause wild and uncontrollable swings in exchange rates. But, as these would be in the interest neither of the oil countries nor of the industrialized countries, Central Banks could expect some co-operation in countering speculative switching of currencies by recycling funds and ensuring that speculation was made much more expensive and risky.

A third course would ostensibly be for surplus holders to invest in non-perishable commodities, including metals. This might drive up commodity prices considerably and add further to the balance of payments problems of the advanced industrial countries. But the commodity producing countries would then be in a position to increase their imports from the advanced countries. This would amount to a transfer of real resources from the advanced industrial countries to the primary producers. The former would have to supply more export goods in order to obtain the same volume of import goods as before. In the process, the balance of payments deficits of industrial countries would be reduced, by reducing their consumption levels.

In fact, however, oil revenue surpluses will be far too large to be absorbed in the purchase of commodities. A minimum annual investment fund of $60,000 mn would very quickly drive prices to levels completely unrelated to any physical basis in production costs or market demand. Prices would then become vulnerable downwards, and governments investing in commodities would stand to lose heavily. Only if the oil producers indefinitely accumulated commodities, with no immediate prospect of using them, would the policy embarrass the advanced countries. Ultimately, however, there would have to be releases from such a stockpile. This would represent an even more dangerous situation for primary producers than that formerly created by the United States Government's stockpile, and producers would no doubt take steps, therefore, to prevent it.

It follows, in practice, that if funds are accumulated by oil producers, they must either be placed on the capital markets of advanced industrial countries or be spent on goods made by such countries.

Either way, the balance of payments problem for those countries disappears. Indeed, it is fortunate for the advanced industrial countries that so large a part of oil production is in the hands of states which are believed to be unable to convert their excess of funds into import goods and must instead lend them back. These unspent oil revenues make it unnecessary for countries to settle their oil deficits entirely within their current trade accounts or by drawing on reserves. They can thus adjust to higher oil import costs over a period with less disruption and probably less loss of real resources. Since they will have to pay interest and may ultimately have to repay the capital in full, these loans cannot be used simply to maintain levels of consumption not justified by the basic conditions of their economies. They should be used to increase investment, yielding returns in terms of real resources which are at least equal to the effective interest charged by lenders. Otherwise the loans will only ease present conditions at the expense of the future. At the same time, refusal to borrow to deal with oil deficits could cause more serious disruption in the present. While individual countries may be able to eliminate their oil induced trade deficits through demand management, export drives or trade restrictions, it will not be possible for all oil deficit countries to do this; their attempts would only result in beggar-my-neighbour policies such as prolonged the slump between the wars. The wisest course, therefore, will be for oil deficit countries to use oil revenue loans to achieve desired levels of investment without making undue inroads into current domestic consumption. The future costs of repayments may be mitigated by changes in circumstances and in terms of trade. Consumption changes may well reduce the price of oil relative to manufactured goods once again, which will make eventual repayment easier. What emerges, in fact, is that the real losers from the balance of payments standpoint will be not the advanced industrialized countries, to which surplus oil revenues will naturally flow, but the non-oil-producing developing countries, which can expect little in the way of capital from or exports to the oil producers.

Leaving the balance of payments effects, the next argument to be examined is that, since far larger quantities of real resources—capital equipment, labour, etc.—will need to be invested to obtain oil from coal or shale than would have been needed to obtain it from traditional oilfields, fewer resources will be available for other activities, thus reducing general consumption in the long term.

In the previous chapter we calculated that the oil 'gap' to be filled from 'unconventional' sources could be 200 mn tonnes per annum by the early 1980s. The capital cost of producing each annual tonne of oil from shale, tar sands, or coal (syncrude) is probably $100, implying a total investment of $20,000 mn by 1980. In 1971, the world oil industry invested $21,000 mn, of which only $7,000 mn was in production facilities. To achieve a cumulative extra total of $20,000 mn within the next 6 years implies an extra $3,500 mn per annum—i.e. a semi-permanent rise of 50 per cent in the investment in production facilities, but less than 20 per cent in total investment. Such an additional burden is hardly intolerable financially. Nor would it have a seriously depressive effect upon general levels of consumption. The fact is that, at present, barely 1·5 per cent of world resources are devoted to winning energy. Even if this were to treble, it would pre-empt only one year's growth in world output. If this burden were spread equitably among the countries of the world, according to their abilities to meet it, the oil problem would in fact be a nine days' wonder. The very essence of the problem, however, is that the benefits of a 'tighter' oil market must accrue to a tiny minority of the world's population, in a handful of countries, while many millions of people in resource poor developing countries like India seem destined to bear a disproportionate share of the burden. At least in the short and medium terms, the oil problem is thus not so much one of resource availability as one of resource distribution.

If the most damaging cost effects of a scarcity of resources bear upon the resource poor less developed countries, this does not mean that the developed countries face no difficulties of their own. Even a temporary disturbance in resource supply presents problems for an industrialized country if it involves a change in the pattern of raw material consumption. The complex and capital-intensive 'round-about' processes of production which characterize the industrialized economies make adjustment costly and complicated. In the characteristic industrialized economy, durable equipment is applied to raw materials—in particular mineral resources—in order to produce intermediate goods, to which more equipment is applied, perhaps in several stages, before the original raw material is in a suitable form for consumption. The durable equipment has itself been produced from resources in the past, and the economy's stock of equipment, which we may for convenience term the capital structure, must be taken as given at any point in time—although its composition is the result of a host of decisions taken in the past, when relative prices of various raw materials may well have been different.

This type of economy is heavily committed to a particular pattern of raw material supply. However, the weight of the commitment does not depend only on the size of the capital stock in the economy but also on how rapidly such capital is normally replaced. In an economy like that of Japan, with a high investment ratio and high standards of obsolescence, this occurs rather quickly. When capital stock is thus being 'turned over' every five years, a country is better placed to adapt than when this happens only once every ten years or so (as in the United Kingdom). Where capital is relatively durable, any changes imposed by raw materials constraints may not be able to be handled by normal replacement investment but may require special 'extra' investment coming out of exports or consumption. Even in 'high obsolescence' countries, some extra investment may be necessary, because replacement rates will vary from one industry to another. The speed of change versus the speed of the consumer's reaction is thus vital: ironically, the most resource-wasteful economies with the most rapid obsolescence rates may find it least troublesome to adjust to resource scarcity.

A second source of adjustment inertia stems from the fact that, in the characteristic industrialized market economy, decisions about a transition from one situation to another (say, from a cheap-oil to a dear-oil situation) are not co-ordinated in any systematic way. In such a decentralized economy, firms are not required to be informed of developments throughout the economy: it is enough that they adapt to the input and output prices they face in such a way as to maximize their profits. Although this works well enough (from the point of view of efficiency, if not equity) in times of reasonably stable prices, it is not necessarily designed to meet the challenge of rapid and permanent changes in relative prices.

It may be objected that firms do not operate in complete ignorance of future prices, and, to the extent that they anticipate them correctly, will begin to adapt their durable equipment in good time. This may be true of the firms immediately affected by the price change, but it is unlikely to be true of the firms that supply machinery to those firms, the firms that supply this second group of firms, and so on, since the future pattern of prices faced by any firm depends on the actions of other firms many stages removed from it.

To take a concrete example, it is instructive to look at some effects of the current rise in the price of oil. Motor firms are currently designing smaller and lighter cars which will economize on petrol. If such cars are to be mass-produced, new machinery will have to be installed on a large scale and there may well be a demand for lighter metal alloys for car bodies which may lead to a higher demand for aluminium. However, investment decisions at this second level (i.e. in the machine tools and aluminium industries) may be deferred until the car firms have made *their* decisions. This process can be traced back to firms progressively 'further' (economically) from the car firms, with less and less apparent connection with them. At the same time, it may be relatively easy and quick to make adjustment at one stage of the process but difficult and lengthy at others. Differing lead times could lead to random, unpredictable bottlenecks, not perhaps in the obvious places (such as in designing cars that economize on fuel or in expanding aluminium output) but in some intermediate stage. Nor will the money market, the instrument by which individual saving and investment decisions are co-ordinated, act to offset distortions in the adjustment process. The immediate tendency of a rise in the price of raw materials will be to lower the level of consumption, in reaction to which consumers, in an attempt to maintain their current standard of living (e.g. by driving as many miles as previously using more expensive petrol) will probably save less of their income. This may make it more difficult for the firms far removed from the oil sector, which should be investing in new equipment, to raise finance for investment: the firms immediately affected by the price rise will have first call on any savings that are available, since the profit opportunities facing them are hardly open to doubt. Government will have to take macroeconomic action to restore savings levels—perhaps adding dangerously to cost-push inflation by increased taxation.

What emerges from this discussion is that change in industrial economies is not as smooth and costless as economic theory would have us believe. The rapidity of the change is the villain of the piece: a slow and steady change can probably be accommodated without too much trouble, but a doubling in the price of an important mineral (such as oil) over a few years is likely to require a greater change in an industrialized economy's capital structure than can easily be brought about by decentralized decisions. Nor will centrally planned economies be immune from the adverse effects of rising costs of raw materials (whether domestically produced or imported). The economic linkages between the various sectors of the economy may be imperfectly understood by the planners, who are not omniscient beings, and there may be strong political pressures to maintain the flow of certain consumer goods and services rather than to invest heavily in the capital-goods sector, even though the latter decision could lead to a smaller drop in welfare in the medium and long term.

In the context of present economic systems, all change, and particularly rapid change, probably tends to be inflationary. Theoretically, assuming smooth and costless change, a rise in import costs would not be inflationary, since the government would reduce domestic demand, causing prices for some goods produced and sold domestically to decline, and making room for a switch from supplying domestic markets to supplying export markets. Whether this is achieved by demand deflation or by adjusting exchange rates does not particularly matter at the theoretical level. In practice, where change is not smooth and costless, modern economies contain monopoly institutions (trade unions, cost plus pricing systems, etc.) which attempt to prevent nominal incomes from falling. Thus, the only way in which relative incomes and prices can change is through inflation, in which those incomes and prices in declining sectors of the economy simply increase less rapidly than average. The more frequently relative changes are required and the greater their magnitude, the higher the implied rate of 'structural inflation' (which is additional to the real resource costs of change itself). Our general conclusion, therefore, is that, while the 'resource crisis' will not permanently or radically alter relative incomes, as between producers and consumers, it will cause temporary disturbances, the least painful way of overcoming which may prove to be through more rapid general inflation.

National Categories and Policy Options

Six minerals—petroleum, natural gas, coal, iron and steel, aluminium and copper—account for two-thirds of world mineral consumption. Of the remaining one-third, almost half is accounted for by sand, gravel, and stone, which are abundant in all countries and not traded significantly. No other mineral accounts for more than 1 per cent of world consumption. Figure 2 plots various countries' consumption of five principal resources (excluding natural gas) against their production. The diagonal line in the figure joins all points where production equals consumption: hence it is the 'self-sufficiency line'. The further away a country is from this line, the greater its exports or imports of resources will be. For example, Japan is a large net importer of resources, and is, therefore, represented by a point of good way to the left of the self-sufficiency line, while the Middle East oil exporters are well below the line.

If the world were neatly divided between developing exporters and industrialized importers of mineral resources, we would find most countries in either the top left or the bottom right of Figure 2. In fact the centre of the diagram is by no means empty. A number of countries—Brazil, South Africa, Australia, Canada, China, and the

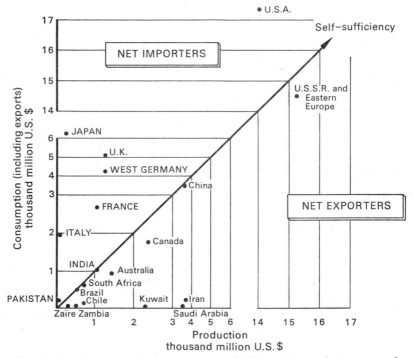

Fig. 2: Production and Consumption of Major Mineral Resources,*
1971.

* Petroleum, coal, iron and steel, aluminium and copper.
Source: Commodity Research Unit estimates.

Soviet Union—are placed close to the self-sufficiency line itself, while the United States, although a net importer of resources, is a large producer in her own right and is, therefore, situated towards the top right of the diagram. Among the developing countries, there are again three groups. One group, distinct from all others, is that of the Middle East oil producers, which export well over 50 per cent of their production. Then come countries rich in non-oil resources, such as Zambia and Chile. Finally, there is the group of unfortunate countries which have neither an advanced industrial base nor a large endowment of resources: several important countries, particularly in the Indian sub-continent, fall into this category. The diagram thus indicates that the conventional dichotomy between resource consumers and resource producers is an oversimplification.

Without going to the other extreme of treating each country as a unique case, it is possible and useful to summarize the anatomy of resource scarcity, as illustrated in Figure 2, by reviewing the situation in which several definable categories of nations now find themselves. Five categories in fact stand out: a category of developing countries with available surpluses of resources, another category of industrialized countries with inadequate resources of their own, a third consisting of countries which, while relatively highly developed, are also self-sufficient from the resources point of view, a fourth composed of those Communist states whose centrally planned and controlled economies set them apart, and, finally, a fifth category of developing nations which have neither sufficient resources for their own needs nor a substantial industrial base. To highlight the economic implications of the resources problem for countries in these separate groups will also help to lay the foundation for our survey, in subsequent chapters, of the political options which each group may exploit.

The Resource Rich Developing Countries

If a less developed country's resources are growing scarce in the world as a whole, their prices can be expected to rise; indeed, some have suggested that their prices are likely to grow at a faster rate than the prices of the manufactures and capital goods imported from the advanced industrialized countries. At first sight, therefore, it might appear that the hope of better terms of trade in the future would encourage less-developed countries to let their resources appreciate in the ground, rather than exploit them. However, although one or two countries, such as Libya, have restrained resource production, most have been inhibited from doing so by the priority which they give to development programmes. Apart from the political urgency of industrialization and development, a substantial proportion of the less developed countries' imports from the advanced developed countries is in the form of capital goods, and any delay in importing them would set back the whole course of development. In other words, a decision not to exploit resources today implies forgoing a whole stream of consumption goods which could be produced using imported capital goods, or even imported directly.

This is the situation of the majority of less developed resource producers. But there is a specially privileged sub-group of countries whose resources can earn more foreign exchange than they can possibly use in their development programmes and which, even though they aspire to industrialization, do not face an imperative economic need to develop a wide range of diversified manufacturing industries, simply because they will always have enough export revenue to import finished consumer goods from the advanced industrialized countries. This is likely to be the situation of some of the Middle East oil states, particularly Saudi Arabia and the Gulf Sheikdoms. Not all oil states are in the same position; Iran, Iraq, and Algeria, for instance, can probably use every cent of export earnings in development and local investment. However, as we have seen, a range of further policy options is open to those less developed countries which do have a potential excess of export earnings, including the use of excess revenues for directly political ends—to influence international diplomacy or to engage in military adventures.

Where reserves of a scarce resource are concentrated in the hands of relatively few countries, economic self-interest will probably lead them to form a producers' cartel such as the Organisation of Petroleum Exporting Countries (OPEC) or—though this is a weaker case—Conseil Intergouvernmental des Pays Exportateurs de Cuivre (CIPEC). Since a complex industrialized economy will react slowly to changes in raw material prices, and only gradually adapt its capital structure to the new pattern of resource availability, such a cartel's optimal strategy would be to force up prices just enough to avoid prompting long-run adjustments, so that the firms immediately affected merely pass on the increases in their short-run costs without altering their fixed equipment. In this way, for example, a large proportion of the advanced industrialized countries' capital stock would remain geared to oil consumption, although on longer-term grounds other fuels should perhaps account for a greater share of total consumption. The line between exploiting consumers' continuing dependence and reducing demand through overpricing is, of course, a very fine one. It may also shift as a result of technological changes which lower the price of potentially competitive resources. The cartel, therefore, has to be managed with considerable skill, and there may be times when it has to reduce prices to pre-empt competition. Whether OPEC will be managed with such skill remains to be seen.

The Resource-Importing Industrialized Countries

As advanced industrialized countries are forced to pay increasingly higher prices for the resources they import, there will be government intervention in the form of encouragement for exploration and development of high-cost domestic resources. North Sea oil and United States shale oil are but two examples. In addition, it now seems likely that there will be government support in most of the advanced countries for technology which can constrain consumption of resources, particularly by recycling metals and increasing the durability of products. However, the long-term shortage of particular resources can only be met by changing the economy's capital structure. Thus government intervention should ideally take the form of encouraging investment in sectors further 'upstream' than those immediately involved in resource shortage. But such radical intervention is only likely to be politically tolerable when the danger signals (high prices) are very clear indeed.

So far, there has been no overall tendency for industrialized countries to experience long-term deterioration in their terms of trade. However, the terms of trade seem certain to deteriorate. Whether this change proves to be a temporary fluctuation, brought on by a high level of demand, or the start of a long-term steady rise in raw material prices, it is bound to put pressure on industrialized countries by stimulating inflation. The economy must forego consumption to pay for more expensive imports. But workers tend to resist this cut in consumption by bargaining for higher wages and businessmen seek to maintain profits. The standard tools of demand management (fiscal and monetary policy) are inappropriate in such cases. They would have to be applied very fiercely, giving rise to unemployment and bankruptcy, at the very moment when the economy should be putting its maximum effort into investment in technological change, resource substitution and resource economies. The economist's standard rejoinder is that, in such a case, a prices and incomes restraint policy is required to prevent trade unions and employers' monopolies or quasi-monopolies from passing on the raw materials price rises in unacceptably high rates of general inflation. The problems of implementing such a policy need no elaboration here. If, however, an alternative attempt is made to cushion the effects of inflation (e.g. by reducing taxation on petrol as has been suggested in the United Kingdom), the role of the price system as a signaller for realignment in production is negated, and adaptation merely postponed. The root cause of the problem is, of course, that all price-rises perform two functions: to take the oil case, internally, they are signals for reallocation of resources away from oil-intensive activities to those husbanding oil; externally, they are the channel by which income is redistributed from the advanced industrialized country to the oil-producing less-developed country.

Apart from their potentially inflationary effect, rising prices of imported resources affect the balance of trade. It has already been suggested that rising costs of energy resources and metals will eventually be passed back to the less developed countries in the form of price rises in the manufactures they import from the industrialized countries. In the short term—defined as the time span in which no major shifts in the industrialized countries' capital structure take place—there is a presumption, however, that the terms of trade will move in the less developed countries' favour. First, there must be a lag between an increase in resource costs and an increase in the cost of manufactures embodying the resource. Second, the less developed countries' imports consist largely of capital-intensive consumption and capital goods; it is because the industrialized countries have the built-up skill and capital to produce these goods relatively cheaply that trade takes place at all. If the less developed countries' development programmes emphasize industrialization via the setting up of industries using indigenous resources, the corollary is that they import goods containing relatively little of their own resources, and built on machines produced long before the price rise they have initiated. Thus the less developed countries' imports are unlikely to bear the full brunt of their own price increases immediately.

In the medium term, during which the industrialized countries are in transition from their old capital structure to a new one appropriate to increased resource costs, a larger-than-usual proportion of their output may be devoted to investment, particularly if the speed of change in raw materials supply is faster than the normal rate of replacement of capital equipment. In an extreme example, oil scarcity might result in the wholesale scrapping of internal combustion cars faster than the rate at which electric cars would normally be developed and marketed. It is likely that the citizens of advanced countries would be unwilling to accept a fall in their standard of living, with the result that resources and goods previously exported would then be diverted to accelerating the pace of development of alternative products. This would lead to a once-for-all deficit on current account, which net private investment from abroad would be unlikely to balance. Although governments could still maintain their exchange rates by running down reserves or borrowing abroad, the current tendency would be to alter the exchange rate, with the intention of discouraging imports and encouraging exports. However, such a devaluation has the effect of making all imports expensive—partly obscuring the relative price rise of the specific resource in question—and thus of opening up other profit opportunities which will seduce funds needed for adjustments in the country's productive equipment. The exchange rate, in other words, is a clumsy weapon which may delay adjustment. Moreover, successive rounds of devaluation may involve resource-surplus countries with investment in the industrialized countries in capital losses, thereby encouraging them to retain their resources in the ground while the industrialized countries are still ill-adapted to a diminished resource flow. More complex fiscal devices, and possible multiple exchange rates, might therefore be a more promising line.

The other method of defending the balance of payments is for an industrialized country to raise the level of its interest rates. This would again have deleterious effects on the transition to a new capital structure. First, high interest rates discourage long-term investments which yield their returns in the distant future; but it is precisely these investments that need to be encouraged if a successful transition is to be made. Second, foreign investors may have a high preference for liquidity, for fear of devaluation or political control of their funds. The only way that enough foreign money can be induced to flow in to maintain the balance of payments equilibrium is to raise long-term interest rates: only then will less developed country investors forego the liquidity they seek. Companies in developed countries would then be faced either with paying very high rates for long-term funds, or going in for short-term 'rolled over' financing: that is, the financing of long-term investment with continually renewed short-term loans. One can foresee tensions and problems (and perhaps also profit opportunities) for financial institutions in these developments.

The Non-Communist 'Independents'

This group of countries consists of industrialized countries which are self-sufficient or net exporters of most mineral resources: the important members are Canada, Australia, New Zealand, and South Africa. These countries differ from less developed country resource owners in possessing an advanced industrial base. Although their resource endowment may have been useful in the process of indus-trialization, their economies are now mature enough not to rely solely on domestic mineral resources; the mineral extractive sector only accounts for 3 per cent of GNP in Australia and Canada, and only 9 per cent in South Africa; compared with 54 per cent in Saudi Arabia and 37 per cent in Zambia. Their economic structure tells us something about the way in which they will act and the policies they are likely to adopt. Because their economies are already developed and diversified, the independents are less concerned than the less developed countries to create 'forward linkages' from their indi-genous resources (e.g. from crude oil production to the refining and petrochemical industries, or from copper mining to semi-fabricat-ing). They will, therefore, be prepared to enter into long-term contracts to supply industrialized resource-importing countries with unprocessed minerals, although this should not be taken to imply that they will be any less economically nationalistic than the less developed countries—indeed, Canada and Australia have recently shown themselves to be particularly nationalistic.

In the long term, the independents' trade balance with resource-importing countries is also likely to differ from that of the less developed countries, chiefly owing to the different composition of their own imports. The process of economic development is char-acterized in its early stages by heavy investment in infrastructure coupled with imports of a wide range of manufactures: this is the stage reached by many less developed countries. At a later stage, when the country's infrastructure is built up, a sound industrial base is founded upon imports of heavy capital goods. The independents are currently at this stage. Whereas, Iran, say, imports a great deal of road-making and excavating machinery, Australia imports a far higher proportion of machine tools and specialized machinery for various industries. The relative importance of capital goods in the less developed countries' import bill has the effect of insulating them in the short run from the effects of their own price rises. Even the manufactured goods they import will tend to be those embodying relatively little of their own resources. Thus the less developed countries should have a surplus on current account. The case of the independents is different, both because their consumption patterns are similar to those of other advanced countries and because their manufacturing industry will use imported materials as well as indigenous materials. Although their export earnings from raw materials will rise, so will their bill for imports of materials and for goods incorporating recently produced raw materials. This will lead to a more even balance of trade between resource-deficit industrial countries and the independents.

On the internal economic front, where the independents bear a stronger resemblance to the advanced resource-deficit countries than to the less developed countries, there is at least a tentative presumption that the independents will adapt to the long-run problems of resource scarcity more successfully than the former, in that, having indigenous resources, they will not be faced by sudden shortages when foreign supplies are disrupted. As we have seen, such sudden crises may prompt the government of an advanced resource-deficit country to adopt short-term policies inimical to its economy's long-term transition to a less resource-intensive pattern of production. A country with its own resources is in a better position to plan its economy's long-term transition. Admittedly, none of the independents is a large producer of fuel resources. Only Canada is self-sufficient in oil (and will perhaps become an important exporter of fuel in view of its large tar sand deposits). Both Australia and South Africa are currently net importers of energy, although Australia has oil and both have extensive coal and uranium deposits. On the other hand, the independents are important producers of other minerals, as is shown in Table 4.2. The independents should therefore adapt relatively easily to any long-term scarcity (or cost increases) in base metals.

Table 4.2. *Mine Production of Metal Ores in 'Independent' Nations,* 1971 (million tonnes)*

	Production	Percentage of world production
Bauxite	12·54	19·2
Copper	1·01	15·6
Lead	0·83	24·4
Nickel	0·45	67·2
Zinc	1·64	30·2

* Canada, Australia, South Africa.
Source: Metallgesellschaft, *Metal Statistics, 1973.*

The Communist Countries

The Communist nations as a whole are net exporters of the major mineral resources (Table 4.3), and are likely to remain so over the period covered by this study.

Table 4.3. *Net Export Trade Position of U.S.S.R. and Eastern Europe in Major Minerals, 1972*
(*million tonnes*)

	(*million tonnes*)
Oil and oil products	42·00
Aluminium	0·14
Copper	0
Iron ore	8·10*
Coal	7·0†

* 1970 figure.
† Estimate.
Source: *World Bureau of Metal Statistics, 1973 and Commodities Research Unit.*

This takes no account, of course, of trade in minerals between the Communist countries, such as the oil, iron ore, and non-ferrous metals which are exported from the Soviet Union to Eastern Europe (China being largely self-sufficient). The largest item in the Communist countries' net exports is oil, consisting almost entirely of oil exports from the Soviet Union to Italy, Finland, and West Germany. However, even this item only represents about 2 per cent of world consumption (or 3 per cent of world trade). Net Communist exports of coal (4 per cent of world trade) consist mainly of exports from the Soviet Union to Japan, Yugoslavia, France, Italy, and Egypt, and from Poland to Western Europe. Soviet exports of iron ore to Western Europe account for a similar percentage of world trade. This relatively slight involvement of the Communist countries in world trade in minerals is further reflected in figures for total mineral trade. In 1968, their net exports of mineral commodities to the West were valued at $2·7 billion, as against net imports of $1·6 billion. These figures compare with a world mineral trade total of $54·8 billion, so that East-West trade in minerals accounts for under 5 per cent of world trade.

East-West trade in minerals will certainly increase in importance over the next ten to fifteen years. Chief among the projects which may effect this change are the proposed pipelines to bring Siberian oil to the Pacific coast, for export to Japan (and possibly the Western United States), and natural gas to both Japan and Europe. There is no shortage of capital from the energy-hungry West to develop the abundant Soviet fuel sources.

The Soviet Union will probably continue to view mineral exploitation in conjunction with foreign interests as a cheap method of building up the infrastructure of underdeveloped regions, such as Siberia. From the Soviet point of view, there is everything to be gained from the conclusion of large 'package deals' involving the installation by foreigners of whole industrial complexes in return for payment in mineral commodities. This has the advantage of by-passing all the complexities and uncertainties associated with the international monetary system, while leaving the Soviet Government free to take advantage of scarcity when precise terms are negotiated. Thus it is safe to expect the Soviet Union to benefit from a transfer of real income from the West. This transfer may well proceed more smoothly than in the case of less developed countries which are paid in dollars, the value of which in terms of goods and services has become difficult to predict.

From the Western point of view, the main attraction of direct investment in the Soviet Union, which will grow more apparent as developing producers force prices up, is that a reasonably assured flow of minerals can be guaranteed, and at a predictable cost in terms of the initial investment. The disadvantages are presumably chiefly strategic, although the mere fact that large amounts of capital are needed for such investment also means that correspondingly fewer savings are available for other purposes. Probably the first of these other purposes to be dropped is the investment in 'upstream' industries which is necessary for successful long-term adaptation to resource scarcity. Aid programmes are another vulnerable category. In sum, the more an advanced Western country's investable funds are pre-empted by large investment projects in the Communist countries, the smaller the likely investment in long-term projects with uncertain returns.

The Resource Poor Developing Countries

This category includes not only countries such as Malawi and other African states which have an insignificant mineral production, but also—and more importantly—large countries, such as India, which produce enough to be self-sufficient in most minerals, but must import large quantities of certain crucial mineral resources.

Published import statistics may give a misleading impression of a poor developing country's dependence on mineral imports. In the truly under-developed economies, there is so little industrial infrastructure that metals—and *a fortiori* metal ores—will not be imported: there is simply not the smelting and refining equipment available to reduce the ores; nor is there machinery to work the unwrought metal into finished products. Developing countries with a more developed industrial base, however, will import proportionately more metal and ore, hence giving the impression that they are more dependent on foreign supply than truly poor developing countries. There is little that can be done to correct this statistical difficulty, beyond warning against uncritical acceptance of published figures.

The effects of rising resource prices on the resource poor developing countries are not difficult to foresee. They have little bargaining power in the international market-place, and will be forced to accept rises in the price of resources they import from the resource rich developing countries. Moreover, since their demand for basic minerals—oil in particular—is inelastic in the short run, the effect on their balance of payments may be very great.

It has been suggested that the oil imports of developing countries could be kept at more manageable levels by either producing more domestically or switching to other forms of energy. However, substitution takes time, and a transition to a new mode of energy, which would be merely inconvenient in an advanced industrialized country, would set back the course of development in a less developed country by several years—years it can ill afford.

The overall terms of trade are likely to move most strongly against those resource poor developing countries which are in the initial stages of development. They will be hit both by rising energy costs and by increases in the cost of manufactures imported from the industrialized countries which will embody the rising costs faced by their producers. On the other hand, developing countries importing capital goods from the industrialized states and simple labour-intensive consumer goods from other less developed nations will be in a better position, since they will be shielded from the immediate effects of rising prices. Even in the latter case, however, the terms of trade will move against them. The general picture is thus the depressing one of a rather rapid transfer of real income from the resource poor to the resource rich developing countries, either directly or indirectly through the former group's trade with the industrialized nations, which will be anxious to pass on their rising costs.

Note

1. The first Secretary-General of the United Nations Conference on Trade and Development (UNCTAD).

Part Two
The Politics of Scarcity

5 Third world resource exporters

The development of policy

The vast bulk of non-renewable resources traded internationally moves from the developing to the developed world. Moreover, many of the low-cost reserves of these resources are located in developing countries in whose economies resource industries tend to constitute the main—indeed often the sole—component. These main features in the economic geography of resources mark the frontier between the anatomy and the politics of scarcity. There has been a tremendous increase in both the scale of fuel and mineral industry investments and the volume of resource trade in the period since the Second World War. This period has also witnessed the establishment of many independent national governments in formerly colonial territories, and the strengthening of both Third World political self-awareness and—within severe constraints—economic initiative. These political and cultural changes have reacted with the experience of vastly increased resource demands by the rich and influential nations (many of them formerly colonial powers) to produce a powerful mixture of motives, objectives, and policies. This mixture is at the heart of the challenge posed by resource issues to the international community.

A cursory glance at the history of resource industries in the developing world shows that a common characteristic has been the formation of associations or agreements involving either producers alone or consumers and producers. Sometimes the composition has excluded governments and has consisted of companies; sometimes the reverse has been the case; and sometimes both governments and companies have been involved.

The object of all these associations and agreements has been to regulate the market for the commodities in question, either in respect of price or production volume or both. Many primary commodities, especially foodstuffs, have experienced pronounced cyclical variations in price, and pressure from producers to form associations or stiffen up existing groupings or agreements has been stronger in periods of falling prices and weaker in boom conditions.

The participation of developed countries in such international commodity agreements as those for wheat, sugar, and coffee is accepted as part of their aid policy to the parts of the less developed world concerned.

The development of producer country groupings amongst the governments of less developed oil and mineral producing areas has proceeded with the same basic objectives of production control and price raising. Only in oil has dramatic success been accomplished, but this widely-publicized success is now clearly regarded as at least a reference point if not indeed a target by other resource producers throughout the developing world. The story of the Organisation of Petroleum Exporting Countries (OPEC) therefore deserves first mention in our review of resource producer policy.

OPEC

OPEC was founded in 1960 by Iran, Iraq, Kuwait, Saudi Arabia, and Venezuela and has gradually expanded to cover every Third World oil exporter of importance.[1] It was established as a reaction to the oil companies' reduction of posted prices for crude oil (the reference price for calculating government revenue) which was itself a response to the slide in realized oil prices in the late 1950s caused by over-supply.

The basic objectives of OPEC have not altered since the two Resolutions adopted at its first Conference in 1960 linked price and unified action against the companies.[2] Members then agreed to seek to raise prices to previously prevailing levels, to insist on justification by companies of proposed price changes, to stand together in the face of any attempted sanctions by the companies and generally to unify petroleum policies and determine the best means of safe-guarding common interests.

The spectacular success of OPEC in recent years in achieving these objectives has been due not so much to any suddenly increased unity of action amongst its somewhat disparate members. They have always shown an ability to subordinate their differences in the common cause of prices. More important was a remarkable con-fluence of events in the late 1960s and early 1970s. First of all, the supply pressures resulting from the six-day war of 1967 had the effect of increasing the value of short-haul Libyan crude and, more importantly, of making the Libyans aware of the impact of market forces on the value of their crude. This considerably strengthened their hand in their later confrontations with the oil companies in 1970, which fortuitously coincided with an unprecedented upswing in European oil demand.[3] Having seen this demonstration of their potential, OPEC proceeded to accelerate their demands with increasing confidence and authority.

In the early 1960s, OPEC's principal achievement was commonly acknowledged to be the negative one of ensuring that posted prices, and hence their unit revenues, were not further eroded despite the slack supply conditions then prevailing. It was only the dramatic rise in the volume of oil exports (at 10 per cent per annum over the 1950s and 1960s, far exceeding that of other primary commodities at 5 per cent per annum) which caused the major oil producing countries to be considerably better off than other resource exporting developing countries. In unit revenue terms however, they had made little progress—indeed it was not until the late 1960s that they regained the peak levels of 1957 (see Figure 3). This was due to a persistent buyers' market during the 1960s when, despite a steady growth rate in world oil demand of 8 per cent over the decade, productive capacity more than increased in proportion. Much of the increase in output was due to the operation of a number of 'independent' U.S.-based oil companies who had first moved into eastern hemisphere exploration ventures with the objective of supplying their domestic markets. When that outlet was abruptly restricted by the imposition of U.S. import controls in 1959, the independents—who were particularly successful in establishing reserves in Libya—competed hard to enter the European markets in competition with the established major oil companies.[4]

But perhaps the main factor in the dramatic growth of oil output was the tendency for the relatively disunited producer governments to press for higher and higher growth in oil production offtakes, thereby boosting their revenues by the only means open to them. The companies were compelled constantly to produce expansion plans.

One important feature of OPEC as an institution was that it provided a forum which facilitated comparison of producer/company arrangements in different countries. This enabled its members to echo the best features of such arrangements in their own countries, thereby considerably speeding up the process of change in various aspects of their relationships with companies. In this process, the

sixty- to eighty-year agreements of the old concessions gave way to
periods of around twenty-five years for newly-acquired concessions;
it became virtually universal for companies to be obliged to sur-
render up to 80 per cent of their original agreement area within a
fairly tight time limit; arbitration provisions became restricted to
local courts; various forms of government participation were

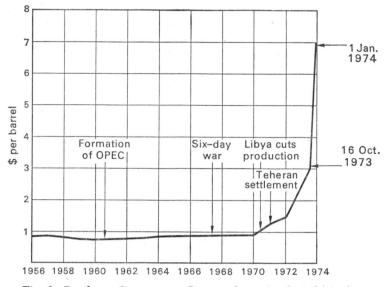

*Fig. 3: Producer Government Income from Crude Oil (Arabian
Light), 1956–74.*

introduced; and there was a general tightening in taxation and fiscal
provisions. Notwithstanding these developments, crude oil prices
and the unit revenue per barrel obtained by the producer governments showed little improvement.

The supply/demand balance underwent a significant change in
1967, when the underlying political unity of the Arab producers was
crystallized during the Arab-Israeli war in June of that year. During
this war—not for the first time—the Arabs used oil as a political
weapon,[5] when all Arab countries banned exports to the U.S. and
the U.K. Since hostilities also forced the closure of the Suez Canal
and the cessation of pipeline shipments to the Mediterranean from
Iraq and Saudi Arabia, Europe suffered some dislocation of supplies.
Re-location of supplies and increased production from non-Arab
sources—particularly Venezuela—averted a major crisis, but the

strain on European supplies was sufficient to send crude and product prices soaring. OPEC had seen a practical demonstration of the supply/demand mechanism, and Libya immediately established an Oil Price Commission to investigate the effect of world oil developments on the price of Libyan oil—a move of great significance in the context of subsequent events.

Nevertheless, it was clear that the Arab producers were still not entirely united, and that the moderates—Saudi Arabia, Kuwait and pre-revolutionary Libya—who also happened to be states solely dependent on oil for their revenues, felt that they were being stampeded into using oil as a political weapon by radicals who were less dependent on oil revenues—Egypt and Algeria. This led in 1967 to the formation of the Organisation of Arab Petroleum Exporting Countries (OAPEC) by Saudi Arabia, Kuwait, and Libya, with the original membership deliberately confined to those states whose sole source of revenue was from oil. Its objectives were regarded as being fully compatible with those of OPEC, within which context the purpose of having a separate Arab Organisation was to co-ordinate the achievement of purely Arab—as distinct from OPEC's multi-nation—objectives. OAPEC's slightly defensive, moderate character was later dispelled when its membership expanded to include virtually every Arab producer of significance. Initially, however, it was seen largely as a commercial and economic union—'the EEC of the Arab oil producers' as Sheikh Yamani of Saudi Arabia described it.[6] Inevitably, however, it progressively took on a political dimension, and it was this body which initiated and organized the production controls of October 1973.

At the beginning of 1968 the OPEC Tax Settlement[7] achieved modest increases in unit revenues by providing for the progressive elimination of certain tax allowances with the ultimate objective of fully expensing royalties. Libya, however, stated that lighter crudes such as Libyan were unfairly treated (the deal had been negotiated by the Gulf States[8]) and declared her intention to seek her own solution to the problem—the first sign of an inclination on her part towards unilateral negotiations, though always within the context of OPEC.

Also in 1968, at the Sixteenth OPEC Conference, an important policy statement[9] was issued which reaffirmed and elaborated on many of the fundamental principles underlying relations between producer governments and concession holders. Most important of these were—that member governments should exploit their hydrocarbon reserves directly, if possible, but if they required the assistance of foreign capital and expertise they should seek the greatest measure possible of participation; that governments should draw up detailed conservation legislation to be followed by all contractors within their territory; and that posted prices, which were to be determined by governments, were to 'move in such a manner as to prevent any deterioration in their relationship to the prices of manufactured goods traded internationally'. Over the next few years OPEC was to achieve the realization of all these aims, and the rôle of Libya in this achievement was of particular interest.

In 1970, the year following the Libyan coup, Colonel Qadhafi Chairman of the new Revolutionary Command Council, opened discussions with the oil companies on prices by threatening reductions in output. Some months later, as no progress was being made in the price discussions, successive production cuts were imposed on several companies. This was ostensibly in accordance with its recent petroleum conservation legislation but, significantly, occurred shortly after discussions with a visiting delegation from Venezuela, who had long been advocates of the use of production controls as a means of regulating world prices.

It was at this point that world events started to turn in Libya's (and hence OPEC's) favour. The Libyan cutbacks, plus the temporary shutdown of TAPline (the Trans-Arabian Pipeline, bringing Saudi Arabian crude to the Eastern Mediterranean) caused a tanker shortage and rising freight rates, as long-haul Gulf crudes were brought in to make up demand. This situation alone was sufficient to enhance the value of Libyan oil. Coinciding as it did, however, with an unforeseen upswing in European demand, Libyan oil was at a considerable premium. In the U.S., too, the first rumblings of an energy crisis and of U.S. long-term dependence on Middle East oil contributed to pressure on supplies and associated price rises. Before the year was out Libya had achieved a 30c/bbl. increase in posted price and an increase in the tax rate from 50 per cent to 55 per cent. Almost immediately the Gulf States in OPEC—who had supported Libya's claims and watched their tactics with interest—started negotiations with the companies for similar benefits. These talks culminated in the Teheran Agreement of 1971[10] (and subsequent separate agreements covering short-haul crudes, including Libyan and Nigerian) which acknowledged, and to a considerable extent met, most of OPEC's long-standing complaints. In addition to the agreed adjustments to posted prices, escalators were built in to take automatic account of inflation (inadequately in the event) and of freight rate fluctuations.

One eventuality not explicitly catered for in the Teheran Agreement was the wide fluctuation in monetary values which occurred in 1971, and in particular the devaluation of the dollar, the currency of posted prices. Since the concept of the Teheran Agreement had been to preserve the real value of OPEC governments' revenues, and since currency fluctuations posed a threat to this, the Geneva Agreement,[11] which was effectively a supplement to Teheran, was concluded in January 1972. This compensated the governments for the loss of real revenue sustained in the recent currency realignments and provided an automatic mechanism for making similar adjustments in the future, by reference to an index of 'key' currencies.

After their success on the price front, OPEC turned almost immediately to another long-standing ambition—participation in oil producing operations, whereby a direct share in ownership would enable them to exercise control over all aspects of operations. Before the end of 1971, Saudi Arabia was delegated to head negotiations for the Gulf States.

Control over their oil had been a goal of OPEC since the beginning, but in the difficult marketing conditions of the 1960s even radicals such as Iraq acknowledged that serious obstacles existed. By 1972, however, the situation was quite different. The discussions on participation then took place against a background of upward movements in oil prices and increasing debate about an impending energy crisis. In this climate, the principle of participation was not seriously challenged by the companies. The talks therefore centred largely upon such points as the initial level of participation, the timing of the progression to higher levels and the compensation terms to be awarded. There was also discussion as to how much of their newly-acquired equity oil the governments should market themselves. Provision was made for any quantities not required by them for direct marketing to be sold back to the companies at prices close to the then market price. This was designed to ensure that most of the profit on this oil went to the governments, with the companies receiving effectively a small commission for marketing the oil on their behalf. This category of oil was termed 'buyback oil'. Finally, at the end of 1972, a General Agreement[12] was drawn up by the Gulf States (excluding Iran and Iraq) and the companies, although not all the states subsequently signed it. This set out a complex schedule for a progressively increasing level of participation, with the States' equity share starting at 25 per cent in 1973 and then increasing over the period 1978–82 to 51 per cent. That the Gulf States still took a cautious view of their own ability to market oil directly was evident from the final agreement which for 1973, the first year of operation, left them selling all but 10 per cent of their newly-acquired equity oil back to the companies.

On the participation issue there seemed to be less unanimity within OPEC than there had been on the pricing issue, and there was even some speculation that the cartel might be disintegrating. While negotiations were progressing, Iran withdrew to make a separate deal with the Consortium[13] and Iraq nationalized her Northern Kirkuk field (with export pipeline outlets in the Mediterranean). Following the Gulf States deal, Nigeria subsequently negotiated a higher initial level of participation (35 per cent) and Libya, which had already expropriated B.P.'s concession holding, indicated that she would be satisfied with nothing less than an immediate 51 per cent. It is true that as 1973 progressed the Gulf States who had signed the General Agreement expressed increasing discontent with their deal and in the process they referred approvingly to the alternative deals obtained by other states. Nevertheless, their discontent derived less from the details of the deals in question than from the continued acceleration towards a sellers' market for oil. The General Agreement had been designed for a buyers' market, and it was not until the Arab Gulf States saw the convincing emergence of the converse condition in the course of 1973 that they began to question its relevance. A totally different type of deal by a major power like Iran could have proved disruptive, but a few months after the signing of the General Agreement she ultimately settled for a purchase and sale arrangement[14] which was designed specifically to give her financial equivalence with the terms enjoyed by the countries which had signed the General Agreement. Without compromising the latter this provided her with a distinctive, non-Arab arrangement which also recognized that Iranian oil had technically remained nationalized since 1951. In return, the companies received security of supply in the form of guaranteed access to slightly larger quantities of oil than they would have had under participation terms. Although technically a purchase arrangement, the purchase price effectively equated with the companies' average crude costs in their participation concessions.

In Libya too the situation represented a potential threat to the General Agreement. The Government had obtained swift agreement from the American independents (with no Gulf interests to protect) to 51 per cent participation, and issued an ultimatum to the majors to agree to similar terms or face immediate nationalization. All the majors unanimously refused since they could not prejudice the General Agreement. The Libyan Government then decreed 51 per cent participation and in some cases followed this up with 100 per cent nationalization. (In March 1974 Shell, for example, was declared nationalized.) However, in the context of the many other events which have conspired to threaten the stability of the original Gulf States deal, the Libyan position in itself cannot be regarded as of primary significance.

The first indication that the days of the new participation arrangements were numbered came in February 1973 when Abu Dhabi, one of the smallest and least commercially experienced Gulf States, became the first to sell her participation oil, and at a record price. The customer was a small Japanese company, and in the following months a host of small independents vied with one another to obtain oil from the National Oil companies. In conjunction with a continuing buoyant demand, and with no international co-ordination between consumers, this resulted in prices being bid up in an auction-type atmosphere. When Saudi Arabia sold her first participation oil in May 1973, she realized $2·55/bbl. on Arabian Light—an increase of about 40 per cent above the May 1972 market price. As market prices soared, there was growing resentment among the producers at the widening discrepancy between the prices they were realizing on their equity oil and those obtained on the bulk of their oil which they were selling back to the companies under the terms of the recent agreement. The negotiated prices for these volumes of 'buyback' oil were on rigid cost-plus formulae and although they had been reasonably close to market prices prevailing in December 1972, when the agreement was signed, the dramatic change in market conditions in the first half of 1973 meant they had fallen well behind current prices.

The rapid escalation in market prices also led to increasing dissatisfaction on the part of the producers with those provisions of the Teheran Agreement which determined their tax revenues from the companies' share of oil. This had included provision for posted prices to reflect general inflation of only $2\frac{1}{2}$ per cent per annum. Even allowing for the other escalation provisions in the agreement, this was manifestly out of line with prevailing and forecast trends. Producer countries therefore judged that companies must be making 'excessive' profits.

By September 1973, therefore, negotiations were under way on two fronts—the raising of posted prices and the revision of volumes and prices on buyback oil. It was also around this time that Saudi Arabia began to indicate that, although hitherto moderate on the use of oil as a political weapon, she was now prepared to consider its use not only for political, but also for economic, ends. On the political front, King Faisal said that it would be 'extremely difficult' for him to go on supplying the oil needs of the U.S. in the face of its continued 'complete support of Zionism against the Arabs'.[15] Although this was not an entirely unpredictable stance, what did surprise the western world was to be told that even Saudi Arabia, with the world's largest oil reserves, was worried about their depletion. As Hisham Nazer, the Minister responsible for planning, pointed out, their 150 billion barrels would be exhausted in 18 years if they sustained the 20 million barrels per day production rate which was the long-term level required by the developed countries.[16] Since Saudi Arabia's revenues at these levels would be far in excess of her requirements, the clear inference was that self-interest alone would dictate reduced production levels to conserve resources: some form of incentive would therefore be required if Saudi Arabia was to produce oil above the level dictated by her own needs. The sort of economic incentive required of the western world appeared to be assistance towards rapid industrialization, to give Saudi Arabia alternative sources of revenue in the post-oil era. (However, at current price levels, it is difficult to conceive even the most ambitious of industrialization programmes being able to absorb Saudi revenues at production levels at or above 20 million barrels per day.)

It was not long before the threatened oil weapon was wielded on political grounds. Within two weeks of the outbreak of the Arab-Israeli war in October 1973, OAPEC (now ten members strong)[17] met and decided to reduce production progressively by a minimum of 5 per cent a month in relation to September 1973 levels and to ban all shipments to the U.S. until the U.S. modified its pro-Israeli stand and the Israelis withdrew from all the Arab territories occupied in June 1967. Only Iraq dissociated herself from the production cutbacks, although her solidarity with OAPEC's aims was clear from her prior act of nationalizing the U.S. interests in the IPC. Group—an action which increased her revenues rather than decreasing them as production cutbacks would have done.

On the day before the decision was taken to cut production came a brusque statement[18] to the effect that the Gulf States had decided to post prices unilaterally. This had been done for some time by some OPEC members—Venezuela, Indonesia, and Algeria—but was a complete departure from previous practice for the Gulf States. The increase in posted prices was an unprecedented 70 per cent, from $3·01/bbl. to $5·11/bbl. for Arabian Light. Also unprecedented— though long advocated within OPEC—was the stated intention that in future 'actual market prices' would determine posted prices, and a fixed relationship between the two was introduced.[19] This was designed explicitly to prevent the situation of the last months, whereby, despite the upsurge in market prices, governments derived no additional benefit on a large part of the oil, which was still 'owned' by companies. This occurred because government take on this oil (in the form of tax and royalties) was based not on actual market prices but on posted prices, which were independently defined reference points.

For a time the majors observed the OPEC-defined market prices since to increase them would have precipitated an upward spiral in posted prices and hence the tax-paid cost of their equity oil. Independents, however, were not constrained by these considerations, having for the most part no equity shareholding in OPEC concessions. Nor had consumer country governments felt able to take any action to control the rise in prices. Consequently, in the increasingly constrained supply situation which followed progressive cutbacks, independents were prepared to pay almost any price for crude oil— particularly for non-embargoed, destination-free crudes such as Nigerian and Iranian. The climax of 1973 prices was reached in mid-December, when Iran's auction oil was sold at prices ranging from $9 to $17 per barrel. These record prices were viewed with particular apprehension by the industry since it was known that OPEC was currently considering further posted price increases for 1 January 1974, and record prices such as these could serve only to inflate their expectations. Nevertheless, when the increases were announced they were still a shock to the industry—posted prices for Arabian Light were increased to $11·65 per barrel, resulting in a doubling of producer government revenue from $3·04 to $7·00. This was estimated to put the oil consuming nations' oil annual import bill into the $100 billion plus range.

For the first time in increasing posted prices, OPEC introduced the concept of linking their revenues to the cost of alternative energy sources. Thus government revenue on Arabian Light—the reference crude—was precisely calculated to be $7 per barrel, which OPEC estimated to be the cost of alternative energy sources. Although both companies and consumer governments had been advocating this concept as something towards which OPEC might aim by, say the end of the decade, they were totally unprepared for it to be introduced with immediate effect.

In the discussions which preceded the 1 January increase, Iran was reputed to have taken a dominant stance, still under the influence of her recent $17 realizations, and even to have pressed for higher prices than were finally agreed on.[20] She met with strong opposition, however, from Saudi Arabia, whose Oil Minister, Sheikh Yamani, had at the end of 1973 undertaken a tour of the major consuming countries to discuss the effect of the oil embargoes and cutbacks. This tour apparently brought about a profound change in his—and Saudi Arabia's—view of price levels.

In November 1973, it was reported that he had warned that 'The price of oil will jump beyond your imagination in 1974 because it is dictated by supply and demand'.[21] After his tour, however, at the December OPEC meetings he was much more moderate. In a public statement made before the new prices were announced he made the point that the Iranian auction oil prices reflected—ironically—the measures taken by Arab producer countries, and Iran had benefited correspondingly in selling her embargo-free oil. Because the unique supply position resulted from political, and not economic factors, he agreed it should not be used for economic purposes. 'If we were to take these prices as a basis for revising Gulf postings we would ruin the existing economic structure of the industrialized countries, as well as of the developing countries. . . . We must be reasonable and act responsibly as members of the international community.'[22] It was presumably a crystallization of these attitudes which led Saudi Arabia to call for a reduction in posted prices from their 1 January level at the next quarterly meeting of the OPEC Economic Committee in March 1974. She was in a minority of one, however, and although she did not succeed in reducing posted prices, her threat to reduce Saudi Arabian postings unilaterally, if the other OPEC members carried out their desired increases, was sufficient at least to freeze them for three months at January levels.

OPEC Stability

The outstanding issue both for OPEC and for those affected by its actions concerns OPEC's long-term stability and capacity to continue to respond to world developments in a concerted way. There are certain aspects on which there continues to be complete unity—for example, on the ultimate goal of full control of oil producing operations, and on the need to industrialize the economies of OPEC member countries in preparation for the post-oil era. Against this, however, must be set the division of views on pricing already mentioned and, more strictly an OAPEC issue, on differing attitudes to the use of oil as a political weapon.

On the first issue, of full ownership of oil producing operations, it must be said (August 1974) that the position is not yet finally resolved. The Gulf states were quick to express their open dissatisfaction with the General Agreement's gradually increasing 25 per cent level of participation, and are currently operating at a higher level (60 per cent). As far as full 100 per cent control is concerned, Saudi Arabia is known to be finalizing a 'new relationship' with Aramco, which is likely to act as a model for the other states. Although the terms of this have not yet been disclosed, the Saudi Arabians have continued to maintain that there is a place for the major oil companies in producer countries' operations, if only for their technological expertise. This would seem to argue for the companies retaining some modified form of their previous concession arrangements in exchange for their expertise, rather than for outright expropriation.

Full control over all their output would be the logical sequel to OPEC's recent history. It would also have the advantage of permitting a wide variety of interpretations by individual OPEC members. It would manifestly satisfy the more radical members, such as Libya, where popular appeal is necessarily a high priority in any action, whilst still accommodating a moderate interpretation on the part of, say, Saudi Arabia, in continuing constructive relationships with the oil companies. There is no reason to suppose that varying interpretations of 100 per cent ownership need constitute a threat to OPEC's unity, since for several years it has embraced a diversity of individual arrangements, including nationalization in Algeria and a unique production sharing arrangement in Indonesia.

The other area where OPEC might be expected to advance on a united front is in the industrialization of their economies. This is a common aim of many OPEC members, both those with surplus revenues and small populations, such as Saudi Arabia and Abu Dhabi, and the more populous states with greater revenue absorption potential, such as Iran and Iraq. They all wish to develop and diversify their economies, thereby gradually moving away from their heavy, or in some cases total dependence on oil. Their first step in this direction is likely to be to establish a greater proportion of the world's refinery capacity in OPEC areas. The *OPEC Annual Review* of 1972 noted that although OPEC countries supplied more than half the world's crude oil in that year, only 7 per cent of the world's refining capacity was located in OPEC countries. Moves to site refineries 'upstream' rather than close to the markets in consuming countries are inherently uneconomic because it is considerably more expensive to ship relatively small cargoes of products over long distances than large crude oil cargoes. Nevertheless, in order to guarantee supplies of oil, many companies are offering to build large refineries in OPEC countries and to incur considerable freighting expenses as a means of obtaining security of supply. Saudi Arabia has received many such offers, and has already concluded her first agreements with major oil companies for joint-venture exporting refineries. By establishing such refineries in their countries, Saudi Arabia and other states hope to lay the foundation for further industrialization, in the fields of petrochemicals, fertilizers, cement factories and so on.

Despite such united advances, however, there are certain dis-unifying forces at work in OPEC and OAPEC. On the use of oil as a political weapon in the Middle East war there had been initial unanimity in OAPEC (with the exception of Iraq, who dissociated herself from the action, though not its spirit). In March 1974, how-ever, when the Arab oil ministers met to discuss its relaxation, two opposing views emerged. The majority view—held by Saudi Arabia, Egypt, Kuwait, the United Arab Emirates, Bahrain, and Qatar—was that a material change had been effected in U.S. Middle East policy and constructive efforts towards a settlement had been made. They were therefore in favour of lifting the embargo with relatively few conditions—i.e., continued efforts towards Syrian disengage-ment and an overall settlement. Three states disagreed, however. Syria would have preferred the maintenance of the embargo until further progress on the Syrian front had been achieved, and Algeria supported her in this view. Libya took the most radical stance, maintaining that any relaxation of the embargo would be premature since no U.S. action to date had warranted it. In the end, the majority of members agreed to lift the embargo but to review the position in June. If by then there had been no tangible progress, particularly with regard to disengagement on the Syrian front, and Israeli withdrawal from the occupied territories, it was agreed that the embargo would be reimposed and possibly more severe measures imposed. Clearly, the potential for disagreement on the extent and severity of the use of oil as a political weapon still exists. So far, the fact that Saudi Arabia and Egypt have both been on the same—moderate—side of the division has served to minimize it. It is possibly only if these two powers were to disagree profoundly that the situation could constitute a major threat to OPEC unity. (Although Egypt is not represented in OPEC, it strongly influences several of OPEC's Arab members.)

The most serious threat to OPEC's unity seems to be on the question of prices. There has been a reported disagreement between Saudi Arabia, who wants to reduce posted prices, and the rest of OPEC, led by Iran, who want to increase them. To the extent that a short and medium term fall in prices, caused by a combination of increased supply resulting from the lifting of the U.S. embargo and reduced demand in response to higher prices, is reflected in disappointing auctions for producer states, it would be difficult for them to justify further price increases in the immediate future. Refraining from further increases in posted prices may be the most that could be expected in the way of price concessions, since the maintenance of posted prices in the face of falling market prices was the cornerstone in OPEC's foundation.

It is true that Saudi Arabia, with her enormous production potential, could make use of the rapid expansion of her productive capacity to ease supply and hence exert an influence on market prices. There are indications that she might prefer to rely on this route, in addition to persuasion with OPEC, rather than resorting to the threat of a unilateral reduction of posted prices. Nevertheless, there are sufficient producing countries with surplus revenues and/or strong conservationist tendencies to offer at least partial resistance to such tactics. The effect on prices of accelerated production by Saudi Arabia could, at least initially and partially, be neutralized by compensating cutbacks in production by, for example, Kuwait, Abu Dhabi, and Venezuela, leaving countries such as Iraq and Iran, who can still absorb their revenues, producing as before. Thus, in the next few years at least it is difficult to see one member, even Saudi Arabia, easily upsetting the intention of the other members to maintain prices. Much depends on the success of oil importing countries—especially the United States—significantly to reduce their consumption and imports of oil. In the longer term, of course—by which is meant 1980 and thereafter—an upper limit will be placed on the price of OPEC crude oil by the emergence in significant quantities of alternative fuels such as coal, oil from shale or tar sands, and nuclear energy.

In the last analysis, therefore, crippling oil prices would impede many of the aims which OPEC countries hold in common, most notably the wish to enlist the developed countries' commercial and technological expertise in industrializing their economies. It may, in the next decade, be this objective which acts as the moderating and unifying force within OPEC.

The Copper Producers

The organization whose name is most usually linked with that of OPEC in speculation about greater solidarity amongst resource producers is CIPEC (Conseil Intergouvernmental des Pays Exportateurs de Cuivre). This consists of Chile, Zambia, Zaïre, and Peru and accounts for 40 per cent of the copper production and 70 per cent of the copper exports in the non-Communist world. Over the past decade, the copper industries in these countries have become, for the most part, government-owned or controlled. The industry provides in each country, except Peru, the major part of natio na export earnings: in Zambia 90 per cent, in Chile 70 per cent, in Zaïre 65 per cent, and in Peru 20 per cent.[24] It has been suggested that the origin of CIPEC owes much to the personal association of two men of similar religious and political beliefs, President Kenneth Kaunda of Zambia and ex-President Eduardo Frei of Chile.

Following his election success in 1964, the policy of Frei with regard to the foreign-owned Chilean copper industry was to seek national control of the industry while simultaneously raising its productive capacity. The first result of this policy was the negotiation of a 51 per cent Government share in the El Teniente mine of a subsidiary of the U.S.-based Kennecott Copper Company, followed in 1969 by a similar deal with the Anaconda Company.

From the beginning of the Frei Government in 1964, which coincided with Zambia's acquisition of political independence, informal contacts were maintained with Zambia on copper policy. Diplomatic missions were then established and an official visit by Kaunda took place in November 1966, during which the Santiago Declaration was signed calling for a conference of producers. This took place in Lusaka in June 1967 and resulted in the establishment of CIPEC by Chile, Zambia, Peru, and the Congo (now Zaïre). The last named had earlier in the year set up the State organization Gecomin to take control of all the country's mining, previously held by Union Minière. The Declaration called on the Conference to study and act upon five points: copper prices, marketing, foreign capital, the development of skills and an agreed policy of copper production. Immediately prior to the opening of the Conference reports appeared—and were promptly denied—that secret discussions had taken place between Zambia and Chile with the object of seeking a joint production cutback of 10–15 per cent as a prelude to setting future expansion rates and floor and ceiling prices. Kaunda's opening speech[25] called upon governments of copper producing countries to take a controlling interest in their resident mining companies and insisted that the companies should exploit resources only in the general interest of the country. Producer countries should take pricing decisions having considered the interests of both producers and consumers. In the event, no concrete action followed the Conference, apart from the decision to establish CIPEC with the objectives of 'the co-ordination and proposal of individual and joint measures in relation to the international copper market, production processes, the expansion of consumption and any other measure that is designed to obtain legitimate increased revenues derived from copper exports from member countries'. The final communiqué referred neither to price control nor production limitation, which indeed would have been difficult to reconcile with the expressed desire of the Peruvian delegation to treble the country's production within a decade, and increase it by 25 per cent in 1967 alone.[26] From the beginning, therefore, the members of CIPEC did not share common positions on pricing or output policy. In November 1967 the office of CIPEC was established in Paris, prompting Le Monde to remark[27] that the choice of Paris rather than London—home of the metal market—demonstrated the new confidence placed by the developing countries in France.

During 1968 and 1969, the first two years of CIPEC, copper prices were high, and this militated against any concerted attempt to control production or pricing policy. It did not prevent the beginning of a programme of 'Zambianization' in the Zambian economy, whereby foreign ownership over a wide range of commerce was curtailed and a number of major companies were invited to offer 51 per cent of their shares to the state.

In January 1970, this procedure resulted in the Government acquiring a controlling interest in the resident copper companies. These measures were roughly paralleled by those of the Chilean

Government both before and during the tenure of President
Allende. The two processes of nationalization, however, proceeded
very differently. Zambia appointed the former owning companies to
manage the State's mines and sell the copper for a percentage
remuneration on the mine profit and sales revenue. (It was decided in
1973 to change these arrangements in favour of more direct management control by one of the State Corporations which had by then
been established to hold the Government interest in mining and a
whole range of industry and commerce.) Compensation was negotiated by agreement, payment has been discharged, credit has been
forthcoming from international banks and the vital skills of ex-
patriate labour have successfully been retained. Indeed, the copper
companies had offered the Zambian Government a shareholding in
their operations on the occasion of Independence, six years earlier,
but the two sides were not able to agree on terms.

No such smooth transition attended the Chilean action, particularly after the speeding up of the nationalization process following
the election of Allende in 1970. Expertise and capital were not
retained, and compensation disputes were acerbic. One of these may
prove to have been significant for the history of CIPEC. The U.S.
Kennecott Company, seeking adequate compensation for its El
Teniente mine which was fully nationalized in 1971, sought several
court rulings in Europe during 1972 to embargo payment for
Chilean copper shipments from the mine until compensation had
been settled. A Paris court did in fact order payments for one cargo
to be blocked. The effect of this was to provide a 'political' focus for
solidarity in CIPEC at the precise time when unity over a joint
economic policy on copper production was undergoing strain.
Copper prices had tumbled during 1970 and were to remain depressed until 1973. This had caused CIPEC to meet to discuss means
of remedying the situation, but a split had developed between the
South American ambition to increase production and the African
desire to restrict production and thereby force prices up. The
Kennecott dispute provoked CIPEC to declare that they would not
replace copper on the world market where Chilean copper was
seized as a result of court action.[28]

Meeting in Paris and Santiago in late 1972 and early 1973, CIPEC
statements[29] reflected the widened frame of reference in which they
regarded the Kennecott episode. Non copper producing countries
were to be invited to attend the CIPEC ministerial meetings to discuss 'solidarity and defence' measures. Appeals were made to the

1962 U.N. Resolution recognizing the right of each country to nationalize its natural resources. The Zambian Minister of Mines called for the transformation of CIPEC into a more cohesive force, since short-term measures taken by individual countries were likely to have only short term effect. Governments now had control of their own copper industries but this control had to be translated into real power. The changed degree of control justified a change in the rôle of CIPEC. It was perhaps significant that the increasingly aggressive posture of CIPEC over Kennecott developed simultaneously with the OPEC negotiations on participation and Iraq's nationalization of the Kirkuk oil field of IPC. There is no doubt that CIPEC has been influenced by the development of OPEC policies.

Further encouragement to CIPEC solidarity followed immediately in February 1973 when Rhodesia closed the frontier with Zambia. CIPEC condemned this 'economic aggression' (against the main transport route for Zambian copper exports) and drew up four main measures[30] by which it intended to fight jointly any assault on the copper interests of a member country:

—the severance of contact with the aggressor by other member nations;
—refusal to sell copper to a buyer who has acted against a member;
—joint sales policy by members;
—the channelling of economic aid by members to the victim.

It is extremely difficult to forecast the future development of CIPEC. While the various policy statements indicate a growing sense of unity and a desire for more aggressive action along OPEC lines, there remain many factors which could inhibit or delay the transformation of these ideas into action. The copper producers differ from the oil producers in having proportionately much greater differences in production costs, and in facing a pool of potentially re-usable metal in use in the hands of their customers. The political unity of OAPEC contrasts with the hostility between Chile and Zambia, and between Peru and Chile. The copper producers are generally more populous than the Arab oil producers. Considerable expansions in copper producing capacity are taking place in developing countries such as Papua-New Guinea, the Philippines, Mexico, and Iran which are not members of CIPEC. On the other hand the accession of these countries to CIPEC might accelerate its change of status. Production control to raise prices would be unlikely to stick in these circumstances. The reintroduction of a fixed producer price instead of the pricing system based on the London Metal Exchange quotations has been advocated many times, most recently by Chile in April 1974, but previous attempts have failed. One recently canvassed possibility is to buy up surplus stocks, possibly using finance derived from OPEC. It is interesting to speculate on the possible rôle of Iran in CIPEC. As a beneficiary of OPEC price gains, with a desire and need to industrialize and broaden the base of her economy, and as an owner of important copper reserves, she might be disposed to take a leading part in the development of CIPEC policies, were she to join CIPEC.

The Bauxite Producers

In order to appreciate the position of the bauxite producers it is necessary to recapitulate some basic facts about aluminium. To produce one ton of the metal requires two tons of alumina which in turn is produced from four tons of bauxite, the whole process being highly energy intensive—about 20,000 Kwh per ton of metal in the alumina to aluminium conversion stage, to say nothing about the ore extraction and (largely chemical) alumina production stages. Because of the enormous demands for electricity, aluminium smelters have usually been sited near hydro-electric schemes or have otherwise been conditional on favourable electricity tariffs. Bauxite itself is the name given to the richest grades of aluminium bearing soils, which tend to be concentrated in the Tropics. Poorer grades are to be found throughout the world, but the ratio of raw material and power required per unit of metal produced increases accordingly. Much research is under way into the utilization of alternatives to bauxite, such as kaolin, gibbsite, and alunite, already used fairly extensively in Eastern Europe. Given time, and at a price, there is no doubt that current technology applied to known reserves could provide alternatives to bauxite, if necessary. Pechiney reported in February 1974 that a 100,000 to 200,000 ton alumina plant could be in operation in 1980, based on non-bauxite clays.[31]

Almost 40 per cent of total world bauxite production (nearly half of the non-Communist world total) comes from four less developed countries: Jamaica, Guyana, and Surinam, all in the Caribbean area, and Guinea, on the coast of West Africa. Jamaica was for many years the world's biggest producer, but has now been overtaken by Australia. These two countries could provide the key to future world developments in bauxite and aluminium, and both are greatly affected by world energy prospects.

With some uncertainty prevailing about the future of export markets for Jamaican bananas and sugar, bauxite is the main natural resource on the island, and yet known reserves will probably be depleted in around sixty years. Choosing the best strategy for the exploitation of this resource is thus central to Jamaican economic policy. In one of several respects which show some similarity with the international oil industry, Jamaica is host to a number of the 'major' multinational aluminium companies—Alcoa, Alcan, Kaiser, Reynolds—and two of the 'minors'—Anaconda and Revere. Bauxite production has increased from 8·4 million tons in 1968 to 12·3 million tons in 1972, and the proportion locally converted into alumina from 26 per cent to 48 per cent in the same period. Government 'take' from the industry in the form of taxes and royalties has risen to $J25 million in fiscal year 1972–3, and the bauxite and alumina industry as a whole contributes about 12 per cent of Jamaican GDP.[32]

The main strands of government policy to increase the economic benefit received by the Jamaican community from the industry have been similar to those developed in oil producing countries. Firstly, as high a degree of 'added value' as possible should be transferred to the bauxite while it remains on the island. For several years, the Government has granted new bauxite mining licences only on condition that the new bauxite is converted locally into alumina. Conversion enhances considerably the input of the industry to the local economy. It has been estimated that one ton of alumina gives twice as much revenue, four times as much foreign exchange and four times as many jobs as one ton of bauxite. It is a long-term aim to raise the proportion of bauxite converted to alumina to 100 per cent, and to go further and establish a smelter to complete the process. Parallel with this, the financial contribution of the industry to the national exchequer has been improved, with government-set transfer prices for alumina shipments from company affiliates to their parents. In face of the pressure for agricultural land, the Land Development and Neutralisation Commission has successfully insisted that the aluminium companies should not sit on land not being put to productive use. After mining operations, it has also been ruled that the land be returned to the state in good condition for agricultural use. Jamaica has also been considering what measures would best satisfy the desire for a greater national say in the affairs of the bauxite and alumina industry. In 1971, following a visit by the Guyanese Prime Minister Forbes Burnham to Zambia, Guyana nationalized the Demerara Bauxite Company, a wholly-owned subsidiary of Alcan, and the question has remained open ever since whether Jamaica should follow suit. Jamaican government spokesmen have been consistently critical of Guyana's action, arguing that it would scare off foreign investment. In a speech at Alcoa's plant in 1973, the Prime Minister, Mr. Manley, is reported[33] as saying that it was important that foreign enterprises came under Jamaican ownership in a participatory sense. But he did not give a high priority to equity participation in existing operations, favouring instead the creation of new joint venture enterprises.

IBA

The establishment of a local bauxite exporters' association—the 'Caribbean Bauxite Commission'—had been advocated for many years by Guyana. It would negotiate jointly with the companies on such matters as higher transfer prices and rates of taxation. Following a period of Jamaican coolness to this proposal, the principle was endorsed in a speech[34] by the Jamaican Minister of Industry in July 1972. He referred to the need for Caribbean producers to co-operate with one another along OPEC lines, while at the same time discounting the possibility of Jamaica nationalizing its industry. A meeting of world bauxite exporters was held in Belgrade during 1973 and a draft agreement drawn up for the establishment of an inter-governmental bauxite association. The International Bauxite Association (IBA) was established at a further meeting in March 1974 in Conakry, Guinea, attended by the Caribbean producers, Guinea, Sierra Leone, Yugoslavia, and, notably, Australia. Addressing the Conference, the President of Guinea summarized his policy aspirations for the producers.[35] He called for the creation of an international Association, the adoption of a policy of local processing, and the achievement of solidarity so as to extend help to those producers who did not possess the means of processing. As far as consumers were concerned, the industrialized nations should continue to obtain the raw materials they required on fair terms. But he stressed that producers called upon to maintain the raw materials supply system should take as their criterion of fairness the mutuality of advantage gained by producers and consumers from the system. The imbalance of advantage in favour of industrialized economies was illustrated by the far superior price ratio for aluminium products against raw aluminium as compared with that between aluminium and bauxite. Hence the emphasis on adding value in the producer countries.

Clearly this Association is likely to grow stronger on the basis of discussion, shared concepts and information, and the issue of orchestrated demands for better tax and price terms and more indigenous processing. The prospects for the bauxite producers emulating the peak of OPEC achievement in jointly controlling production, increasing price, and negotiating participation would depend on four factors: firstly, the attitude to the principles involved of Jamaica and Australia as the 'moderates' in the club; secondly, assuming agreement amongst all producers on the various principles, the achievement in particular of an acceptable method of controlling production; thirdly, a relatively inelastic consumer response; and finally, whether or not action by other resource producers along the same lines was proceeding simultaneously—by accident or design.

The general considerations informing Australian policy-makers in the resource field will be discussed in Chapter 7. The establishment of IBA was welcomed by Australia as being consistent with Australian policy to assist less developed countries (LDCs) to achieve a reasonable return for their resource exports. But it was stressed that this policy included paying due regard to the interests of consumers. The Jamaican attitude on the rightful or prudent extent of 'participation' is also crucial. Relations between the resident aluminium companies and recent Jamaican governments have been good. The companies have sensibly sought to aid the local economy beyond the strict confines of their own operation by establishing model farms and dairies. However welcome this has been, the desire of successive Jamaican governments is still to have a local aluminium smelter. Lack of cheap electrical power has always militated against this; but it is not inconceivable that the establishment of a smelter would meet the requirements of the Jamaican Government for 'participation'. Given that the overall rise in world energy costs has reduced the differential in the economics of site location, a smelter could be more satisfactory to both Jamaica and the companies than anything which might emerge from the multilateral efforts of IBA. Furthermore, Jamaica enjoys a superior bargaining position with the companies compared with the other producers owing to the easy mining characteristics of her deposits and their accessibility for transportation to the U.S. market.

Jamaican deposits lie virtually on the surface whereas those of Guyana, for example, lie under 100 feet of over-burden. On the other hand, the political difficulties for Jamaica in not seeking participation in the industry are not to be underestimated. One example is the situation created by Alcan's acquisition of a share in the Norwegian State-owned aluminium company, ASV. This was consummated on the basis that the Norwegian Government should be represented on the Board of ASV's main source of raw material—which is Alcan Jamaica. It is not easy to conceive that the Jamaican Government will always be content to be apparently less well placed than the Norwegian Government in this important Jamaican industry.

Production control of bauxite and alumina could probably be effective if the five main producers so decreed. But this would probably be a weapon of last resort, failing agreement on improved prices, the location of processing plant, and other productive joint ventures, and would almost certainly be a weapon of much decreased effectiveness after a year or two. Assuming a delayed market price response to hypothetical production cuts, the ability of the producers to sustain the lost revenue would vary widely as between Australia and the Caribbean and African members. The length of delay in price response would reflect the ability of consumer country economies to readjust consumption and bring forward scrap supplies or alternative materials. Given the 20 per cent of aluminium supply which arises from scrap, an initial assessment would cast some doubt on the ability of most producers to sustain the effects of curtailed production. Whether other resource producers would be disposed to synchronize their actions to add leverage to IBA action is possible; but it is not easy to visualize the specific conditions which would bring such a conjunction about. There exists no common link, such as Iran might conceivably provide between OPEC and CIPEC.

Other Producers

Although somewhat overshadowed by developments in oil, copper, and bauxite, producers of other commodities are also increasingly urging co-operative action.

Sri Lanka has called for a ministerial meeting of all natural rubber producing countries to exploit the opportunity created by the drastic impact on synthetic rubber costs of the October/December 1973 oil price increases.[36]

An UNCTAD study[37] has recommended talks on the feasibility of creating an international tungsten agreement. Following a familiar pattern, 60 per cent of 1972 world trade in tungsten ores and concentrates came from developing countries (Bolivia, South Korea, Thailand, Brazil, and Peru) and nearly 20 per cent from Australia and Canada. The EEC, Japan, and the U.S.A. accounted for nearly 75 per cent of imports. Sharply fluctuating demand in the end-use sectors for tungsten—cutting tools and mining equipment—has produced considerable price instability.

An unusual problem is faced by silver producers in less developed countries, of which the most important are Mexico and Peru, accounting for around one-third of world production, excluding the U.S.S.R. A similar proportion comes from Canada and Australia, with the U.S.A., at around 17 per cent, the other major non-Communist producer. Mexico, supported by Peru, has proposed a common front of silver producers to defend the price of silver which had been stagnating between the 1967 high and the increases due to speculation in late 1973 and early 1974. However, at a meeting of the five main producers in 1971, Mexico and Peru were unable to persuade the others to set up an agreement to halt the slide in prices. One problem was that the U.S.A., Canada, and Australia viewed the price situation in a totally different light. For them silver was predominantly a by-product from more important mining operations in lead, zinc, and copper, whereas for Mexico, about 40 per cent of silver was mined as a commodity in its own right; and almost one-third of total Mexican production was accounted for by small concerns to whom low prices could be crippling. Another problem for silver producers wishing to raise or maintain prices has been that there are ample stocks of silver held in a variety of ways, which will undoubtedly find a way on to the market, but in a wholly unpredictable fashion. For Mexico, the irony is that one of the major elements in this uncertainty is a fellow Third World country—India—which, although not a significant producer, has holdings of silver estimated at between 2 billion and 7 billion ounces, much in the form of works of art. In 1970, for example, 35 million ounces reached the London Metal Exchange from India, roughly equivalent to Peru's production in that year and about 80 per cent of Mexico's production.

A Resource Ideology

Resource producers differ markedly both as between members of the same resource organization and between those organizations.

P.S.—4*

Among the various countries there are differences—and disputes—
of politics, race, religion, geography, economic strength, and
development status, to say nothing of the different characteristics of
the resource markets. In many ways it seems odd to generalize. And
yet not only is there virtual identity between many of the specific
demands made by producers of different resources but there are
also close and growing similarities in their overall ideological framework of policy.

Certain specific demands are easily recognizable as being common: increased national ownership and control, increased revenue,
increased local processing, and so on. The tactic of seeking to
increase bargaining power by forming associations has been learned
by all concerned, and each association is now very much aware of
the existence and activities of the others. In developing countries,
almost all disposed towards planned economies, the special rôle of
natural resource industries as being usually the most important
sector and at the same time one based on wasting assets, ensures a
similarity of planning policies.

Underpinning all of this is a less tangible base which unites the
producers while admitting wide divergencies of political philosophy,
as between Zambia and Chile or Iran and Libya. It consists, firstly,
in the belief that political independence is not enough; full nation-
hood requires economic sovereignty. Secondly, there is the mutual
sense óf grievance of the resource exporters, who see themselves as
nations struggling to regain ground lost to them over the years
through what they regard as the unfeeling march to wealth and
privilege by the industrial world. Thirdly, the self-confessed global
failures and weaknesses of the rich countries (Vietnam, inflation,
European disunity) are becoming more than ever apparent to the
producers at a time when control over the supply and price of
resources much needed by the rich seems increasingly, if still partially, to be within their grasp. These three factors have combined to
produce an ideological dimension to policies centred on resources
which is recognizable right across the Third World. It implies a
degree of alignment between Third World resource producers which
falls short of alliance but need not for that reason exclude concerted
policies. It also implies a general politicization of resource negotiations which partly produces and partly feeds upon specific instances
such as the Arab boycott of the U.S.A. and Holland over Israel or
the Chilean threat to cut copper supplies to Britain because of the
new Labour Government's attitude to the regime in 1974. It clearly

implies a virtually irreversible commitment to the maximization within national boundaries of benefits from resource industries. The desire to indulge in cartel arrangements with others against consumers, even with the prospect of some sacrifice in the process, is not to be underrated. But this desire seems destined constantly to meet constraints which are to be overruled only by very advantageous market conditions plus a strong and distinct political focus, as in OPEC. All these implications clearly bear on the rôles, objectives, and choices of the resource consuming and importing nations which will be discussed in the next chapter.

Notes

1. Present membership is: Iran, Iraq, Kuwait, Saudi Arabia, Venezuela, Indonesia, Algeria, Libya, United Arab Emirates, Qatar, Nigeria, Ecuador, and Gabon (Associate Member).
2. Resolutions I 1.2 and I 1.4 of the OPEC Conference in Baghdad, September 1960.
3. Discussed in *Petroleum Intelligence Weekly*, 29 March 1971.
4. Usually taken to refer to: BP, Shell, Exxon, Standard of California, Mobil, Texaco, and Gulf.
5. It was used by Saudi Arabia against France and the U.K. in 1956.
6. *Petroleum Intelligence Weekly*, 22 January 1968.
7. *Petroleum Intelligence Weekly*, 15 and 22 January, 1968.
8. Kuwait, Iran, Iraq, Saudi Arabia, United Arab Emirates, Qatar.
9. OPEC Resolution XVI 90: 'Declaratory Statement of Petroleum Policy in members' countries'. OPEC Conference in Vienna, June 1968.
10. Text printed in Supplement to *Petroleum Intelligence Weekly*, 22 February 1971.
11. Text print in *Petroleum Intelligence Weekly*, 31 January 1972.
12. Text printed in Supplement to *Petroleum Intelligence Weekly*, 25 December 1972.
13. Consisting mainly of the seven major oil companies, operating the largest concession in Iran.
14. Text printed in Supplement to *Petroleum Intelligence Weekly*, 23 July 1973.
15. Interview on NBC TV, 31 August 1973, reported in *Middle East Economic Survey*, 7 September 1973.
16. Address to American-Arab Association for Commerce and Industry, New York, 11 September 1973; text reprinted in Supplement to *Middle East Economic Survey*, 28 September 1973.
17. Saudi Arabia, Kuwait, Libya, United Arab Emirates, Iraq, Qatar, Bahrain, Egypt, Syria, Algeria.
18. OPEC Gulf States Communiqué, 17 October 1973, reprinted in *Petroleum Intelligence Weekly*, 22 October 1973.
19. Ibid.
20. See statements in *Middle East Economic Survey*, 28 December 1973.
21. *Petroleum Intelligence Weekly*, 19 November 1973.
22. *Middle East Economic Survey*, 21 December 1973.

23. See for example statements in *Middle East Economic Survey*, 9 and 16 November 1973.

24. Louis Turner: *Multinational Companies and the Third World*, London 1974, p. 93.

25. *The Times*, 2 June 1967.

26. Conference objectives outlined in *Financial Times*, 8 June 1967.

27. 19–20 November 1967.

28. *Financial Times*, 16 January 1973.

29. See *Financial Times*, 18 October, 2 and 5 December 1972.

30. *Financial Times*, 2 February 1973.

31. See *Financial Times*, 16 January 1974.

32. *Financial Times*, 21 November 1973.

33. *Financial Times*, 21 November 1973.

34. *Financial Times*, 20 July 1972.

35. *Guardian*, 8 March 1974.

36. *Financial Times*, 12 February 1974.

37 Prepared for the Tungsten Consultations, Geneva, 30 October 1973. Reported in *The Times*, 22 October 1973.

6 The consumers

Given a continuance and intensification of the trends in the resource-exporting developing countries, which have been described, what are the circumstances and options facing the major consumers and importers of resources in the industrialized world?

It should first of all be recognized that the formulation of policy options is constrained by the legacy of history. Two elements of this legacy are worth stressing at the start: that produced externally by the historical external relations of the rich countries with the resource producers; and that produced internally by the experience of wealth and growth.

The Colonial Heritage

Fanning out in space and time from the European Industrial Revolution of the late eighteenth century, there have developed in the advanced industrial nations of the West similar mass consumption economies whose momentum drives the international trading system and has intimate interconnections with global political and security issues. With less than 20 per cent of the world's population, the main consuming economies of the U.S., Japan, and Western Europe account for nearly 60 per cent of the world's GNP. All these economies were founded on the processing of raw materials which were at first mainly local and then, with the spread of international colonization and trade, increasingly imported from the 'new' countries. A handful of the latter, especially Australia and Canada, have achieved comparability of prosperity with the major economies; but the majority, in Africa, Latin America, and non-Communist Asia, now account in total for only 10 per cent of the world's wealth, as measured by GNP, although half the world population has come to be situated there.

It would not be productive to enter into the debate on the historical relationship between colonialism and economic interests. It can be said that the two were associated to some degree, although historians of different persuasions may point to particular episodes to illustrate either the manifest rôle of economic interest or alternatively the primacy of political motives. Nor is it relevant here to do other than note that in the long history of colonial investment in raw materials access was obtained sometimes by conquest and sometimes by treaty or invitation. Similarly, access to materials was retained sometimes by force but also by virtue of superior technical and commercial skill, exercised in peaceful circumstances.

The fact remains that over time there were instances of what may charitably be called myopia or with less charity, exploitation, which in conjunction with many cultural changes have effectively made the words 'colonialism' and 'imperialism' into highly pejorative terms which to this day poison the waters of international relations. There is a considerable body of opinion in the developing world which regards much of the developed world's present-day trade and investment as but the old colonialism under a new guise—with the multinational corporation as the villain of the piece. Whatever the merits of the criticisms, industrial resource-importing countries have to reckon with the present-day attitudes arising from an historical epoch in which they had a totally different experience from that recollected by many resource exporters.

The Philosophy of Growth

In the industrial nations there has come about in the course of time a general expectation of continued economic progress. This seems to include the belief that a growth process which has demonstrably survived severe shocks in Europe and the United States can persist indefinitely, and a desire that it should continue to confer its broadly dispersed benefits. In the modern era this philosophy has been refined by the advanced industrial nations into an interconnected set of policies on full employment, industrial development, and technological leadership. This is a world view in which natural resources are there to be used for growth. The question of not using them arises only when technology or economics favours such a course of action with regard to a particular commodity, in which case the general response is to seek a substitute. Furthermore, the question of not using them has seldom arisen—apart from wartime—in anything other than a gradual process of change.

Widespread social expectations of high employment have led industrial governments to produce economic planning systems oriented to continued domestic growth and the viability of important industries and regions. Predicted changes in the pricing or availability of resources will in the first place be evaluated against these objectives. Until recently, the historical experience of the industrial nations has generally been that the unrestricted supply and stable price of raw materials have acted as engines of domestic and international economic development rather than as constraints. As and when this picture changes, the industrial nations may simultaneously face strains in internal economic growth and international clashes of economic interest. Both will place severe demands on domestic social cohesion and the ability to modify community values and expectations.

The Actors and their Situation

The United States, Japan, and Europe account for the vast bulk of the world's consumption of resources. Since 1950 alone they have consumed more materials than the world produced in the whole of its previous history. Table 6.1 shows the consumption pattern for some main resources.

Table 6.1. *Consumption of Major Minerals by Volume by Principal Consumers as a Percentage of World Consumption, 1972*

	% Oil	% Coal	% Steel	% Copper	% Aluminium
U.S.A.	30	18	21	25	42
Japan	9	3	12	13	10
W. Europe	27	14	26	33	22

Source: Industry estimates.

One of the most important features of these two decades has been the growth of a heavy dependence by many industrialized countries on imported resources. Table 6.2 illustrates the overall state of self-sufficiency in respect of the same important resources.[1]

This basic data highlights four facts. First, all the main economic units in the West are significantly dependent on imports for at least some of the basic resources (to say nothing of a whole host of individually less important materials). Second, the United States is

Table 6.2. *Resource Self-Sufficiency, 1972*

	% *Oil*	% *Coal*	% *Steel*	% *Copper*	% *Aluminium*
U.S.A.	69	100	75	91	15
Japan	0	35	27	23	34
W. Europe	3	83	86	28	41

Source: Industry estimates.

comparatively well placed when set against Japan and Western Europe. The advantageous U.S. resource position consists not merely in the generally higher ratios of self-sufficiency which happen currently to have been achieved, but also in a totally superior endowment of resource reserves which remain to be tapped if and when circumstances make it necessary. The massive resource base at the disposition of the U.S.A. has been thoroughly analysed by the National Commission on Materials Policy and is set out in detail in Appendix B. The order of magnitude of known and potential reserves of 68 materials has there been set against an estimate of cumulative demand up to the year 2000. It can be seen that where future demand is not covered by known reserves at 1971 prices, it is covered many times over in almost all cases by additional reserves exploitable at higher prices and/or with improved technology, or by undiscovered but geologically predictable deposits. This gives to the U.S. an ultimate flexibility denied to Japan and Europe.

A third fact to emerge is that Japan represents the opposite extreme to the position of the United States, with Western Europe as a region coming somewhere mid-way. Of all the major industrial powers, Japan has the narrowest domestic base of fuel, raw materials, and food. Her remarkable economic growth has been based on resource processing industries which have rapidly exhausted her indigenous reserves, already severely depleted by the Second World War.

Finally, the figures in Tables 6.1 and 6.2 illustrate the outstanding significance of oil in the international system. Japan is totally dependent on imports; Western Europe is currently not much better placed (North Sea production is unlikely to increase regional self-sufficiency much beyond one-quarter by around 1980); and the United States—though it has been emerging as a substantial oil importer—is still in an overwhelmingly superior position.

The Point of Transition

Japan's progress to the top rank of industrial powers on the basis of a pronounced resource importing and processing economy exemplifies the zenith of the confidence felt by the industrial nations in the international resource supply system. The essential quality of this confidence was a belief that the system was elastic in its supply response to the initiative of consumer demand. Clearly Japan has had little alternative to reliance on imports but this very fact might have been expected to sensitize her, above all other industrial nations, to the dangers of import dependence. It is true that she has diversified her sources of supply for non-fuel minerals, but over 90 per cent of her oil imports come from the Middle East and 44 per cent of her coal imports from Australia. Further, it was only in 1967 that an objective was declared of supplying a minimum percentage of her 1985 oil consumption from Japanese-developed sources overseas—and that proportion was set at only 30 per cent. Although Japan has been to the fore amongst industrial nations in setting up joint ventures with less developed resource-exporting nations, whereby the latter would have an equity stake in the projects, she has not been noticeably in advance of other importers in recognizing the strength of the resource exporters' desire to carry out processing activities. It is true that in the post-war era Japanese foreign policy had to be essentially passive, in both her own interests and those of the United States, and that passivity in foreign relations breeds insulation from relevant political and cultural processes. Nevertheless, when all is said and done, nothing illustrates the past attitudes and experience of rich resource-importing countries better than the founding of the Japanese economic miracle on the historical basis and future expectation of uninterrupted access to foreign raw materials on commercial terms. The evidence presented in Chapter 5 on the less developed resource exporters must lead us to doubt whether such a basis now exists, or will exist for much longer, in quite such a straightforward way.

To put the matter briefly, the industrial resource-importing countries are at a point of transition. Behind them lies an era in the successive periods of which they enjoyed all the privileges associated with real ownership of resources developed under their auspices in colonial territories, or effective ownership through their investments in post-colonial developing countries (as well as in countries such as Australia). Ahead of them lies a situation in which all that seems certain is that their individual initiative in international resource policies will be much more constrained. In the future, a range of relationships is possible both between the industrialized importers

and the developing exporters and amongst the industrialized importers themselves (to say nothing of the other actors we have yet to
discuss). In the meantime, a predicament familiar to policy analysts
presents itself: that life goes on, demanding and obtaining day-to-
day decisions, but that these decisions and their rationale—assembled before or after the event, using good or bad data—go to form
the building blocks of longer term policy positions. The resource
importers are currently in this very sensitive phase, when much that
could make for good or ill in the future is on their agenda of international relations. What they now face are the preliminary movements in a process yet to run its course. Their uninterrupted access to
foreign raw materials on commercial terms of their own choosing is
gone in the case of oil and under strain in the case of others. Given
their historical experience and the imperatives of modern industrial
economies, the first inclination of industrialized resource importers
will be to prepare policy options to mitigate the effect on them of a
situation of restricted resource supply.

Policy Alternatives

In theory, any consuming country or region fearing restricted supply
of a resource traditionally imported from certain sources may
pursue four strategies, separately or in combination:

(a) change to a more liberal source of imports;

(b) reduce or stabilize imports by exploiting available domestic
reserves more intensively, by using technology to develop substitutes,
or by acting directly to reduce demand;

(c) continue to rely on imports from the traditional sources but
enhance the security of their supply by making special bilateral
arrangements with the suppliers;

(d) continue to rely on imports from the traditional sources but
seek a multilateral solution to the supply problem in concert with
other affected importing countries.

The first strategy, which implies going beyond the Third World
resource exporters to 'safer' areas such as Canada or Australia, begs
a question which will be discussed more fully in Chapter 7. Suffice it
to say here that the passive title of 'mineral storehouses' often
applied to Australia and Canada is in curious contrast to the very
active and individual resource policies now being developed there.

The second strategy reflects the fact that the bargaining power of resource importers *vis-à-vis* exporters is partly a function of their possessing both the technology and management skills to produce substitutes for any given resource (or otherwise to reduce demand for it) *and* the ability to rearrange an economy around the new substitutes or methods. The maintenance of economic growth in a situation of resource pressure seems to depend on continued gains in the technology of exploration, extraction, processing, and transportation of ores and oil and increases in the efficiency of energy use.

Underpinning these special technical requirements is the management of research and development (R & D) and the process of general management, and behind that the broader educational system at all levels. Acting simultaneously as a check and a spur to this technological solution is the premium increasingly placed by members of the industrialized societies on the quality of their environment. There is no doubt that the energy and extractive industries, with their large-scale operations, will continue to satisfy demand in the future only as a result of projects presenting environmental problems of a very high order (e.g., open-cast coal mining, shale processing, nuclear generating stations). Acceptable environmental standards can no doubt be achieved, over time and at a cost, by the application of a degree of technical effort and ingenuity commensurate with that devoted to the extraction process itself. It is less certain that the 'technocratic' solution will mollify all the environmentalist groups whose aesthetic principles have recently commanded political support.

The explicit recognition of increasing reliance on technology over a broad front may give cause for concern as to whether there exists a rational system for deciding the level of, and priorities within, public and private R & D programmes—or any very satisfactory means of observing and correcting for declining returns in R & D. The integration of environmental protection objectives into the programmes compounds the difficulty. The increasing size and cost of resource developments may entail an extension of cumbersome joint ventures between companies and countries in the necessary R & D, as well as at the production stage. The simultaneity of major projects throughout the resource industries may result in shortages of men with scarce skills, such as welders. These factors in combination lend an additional quality of unpredictability to the pace and direction of indigenous resource development in the consuming areas.

Bilateralism and Multilateralism

Some of the features and problems of the third and fourth strategies mentioned above are illustrated by the steps taken by oil importing industrial countries in response to the actions of Arab oil exporters in October 1973, which were described in Chapter 5. It is important to note, however, that even before those events forced oil importing nations quickly to rethink their international energy policies, some concern had already been felt about the international implications of the predicted tight balance between long-term supply of and demand for crude oil in the non-Communist world.

One of the major bases for this prediction was the impending emergence of the United States as an important oil importer. From a position in 1972, when imports formed less than one-third of U.S. oil consumption, it was forecast[2] that by 1980 the proportion would have risen to around one-half. The reasons adduced in support of that forecast were many and complex. In brief, domestic U.S. oil and natural gas production was felt to have reached a plateau; plans for nuclear development had not been fulfilled; coal production had stagnated; the environmentalist movement was having a considerable impact on the pace of construction of facilities affecting all kinds of energy; and the whole economy—particularly the private consumer sector—was characterized by a profligate attitude to energy consumption. The upshot was that the United States was seen in mid-1973 and before to be moving irrevocably towards a position where the Middle East oil exporting bloc would supply the bulk of the increase in her energy demand for the next decade. In this, the United States was converging on the positions of the other two main energy consuming blocs in the non-Communist world.

From 1973 to the end of the decade, both Japan and the European Community were expected to increase their dependence on oil as a source of energy: from 77 per cent to 80 per cent and from 64 per cent to 70 per cent, respectively. Japan was already wholly dependent upon imports for this oil. The European Community, on the other hand, was then expected to reduce the imported proportion of its oil requirements from 97 per cent to the still significant level of 75 per cent through the development of indigenous resources, especially North Sea oil. The absolute volumes of imported oil required by Europe nonethless were expected to increase substantially over the period, as were those needed by Japan and the United States.

Even before the 1973/4 oil crisis, therefore, the outlook for the future of the Western oil consuming economies was one of mutual and increasing dependence on oil, and on oil imports, which for a decade or so could be obtained in substantial quantities only from the Middle East. At a financial and technical level, the energy industries were contemplating vast expenditures on exploration for and development of conventional crude oil reserves, as well as of the solid fuel deposits and non-conventional oil reserves in shale and tar sands which, on the demand and price assumptions then reigning, seemed necessary in some degree to supplement conventional crude oil reserves. On an international political level, it was recognized that the scene was set for competition between oil importing nations to secure preferential access to scarcer supplies. This was illustrated in May 1973 in a press statement by the Japanese Industry Minister Mr. Nakasone on his return from a Middle East tour.[3]

I have become strongly aware of the need to approach Middle East oil not simply as tradeable merchandise but something more deeply politically involved. Oil is a critical resource for Japan and dealings in oil cannot be handled by individual Japanese enterprises or traders alone without the support of the Japanese Government and its people. The Japanese Government was not doing enough in the past. The Japanese Government will involve itself in strong and continuous petroleum diplomacy in the future.

The international oil situation is in a period of transition with producing nations seeking partners among consuming nations for long range oil contracts. Establishment of a co-operative relationship between a group of the world's largest oil producing nations and Japan as one of the world's largest consuming nations, will have an important influence over the international oil scene.

After the oil price rises, production cuts, and embargoes of October 1973 such statements occurred more frequently and were followed by action. In early December the French Prime Minister, M. Pierre Messmer, told a political rally that 'Producing countries are interested in getting the largest possible return for their industrialization, and no one can blame them. Therefore, we ask if the effort towards industrialization . . . doesn't necessitate accords between governments rather than between governments and companies.[4]' One month later, on 7 January 1974, the French Government announced that it had agreed to conclude a deal with Saudi Arabia for crude oil supply. M. Messmer stated that, faced with major and lasting rises in the prices of all raw materials,

France's policy must be to establish new supply pacts with producer nations, not only of oil but of all raw materials.[5]

The counter-philosophy, that a multilateral approach by consumers was the only appropriate way to solve world energy problems, had been most forcefully expressed by the U.S. Secretary of State, Dr. Kissinger in a speech delivered in London on 12 December 1973.[6] He advocated setting up an energy action group of the major Western industrial nations to produce a programme designed to deal with energy conservation, new energy sources, the incentives necessary for oil producing countries to increase supplies, and a co-ordinated international approach to energy research. The underlying world oil supply and demand trends constituted a 'chronic crisis' which the Middle East war had made acute. The underlying problem was one that the United States could solve alone, 'though with great difficulty', but one that Europe 'cannot solve in isolation at all'. It did not seem to be an accident that Dr. Kissinger's speech was delivered two days before a European Community summit meeting in Copenhagen. However, the immediate response to the proposals at the European summit was lukewarm and French opposition was particularly marked. In the end, the Ministers 'confirmed the importance of entering into negotiations with oil-producing countries . . .' and further nominated the Organisation for Economic Co-operation and Development (OECD) as a forum for oil consuming countries to study energy problems.[7] Albeit indirectly, they thus chose, in concert, to reject the American advocacy of a new action group of Western oil importers.

The Washington Conference

The American initiative was nonetheless reinforced by President Nixon on 9 January 1974, when he called for an energy conference to be held in Washington in February between the United States, Japan, and the European Community. Between the invitation and the holding of the conference, however, European diplomatic exploration of bilateral oil deals with suppliers continued. The French deal with Saudi Arabia announced on 7 January was followed in the same month by a British barter arrangement with Iran, both accompanied by talk of further and more considerable agreements in the future. West Germany stated its desire for a united Community energy policy but pressed ahead with discussions with oil producing countries, as did Italy and several other oil importing countries.

These events revived the debate about the merits and drawbacks of bilateral arrangements between oil-importing and oil-exporting governments. The arguments against fell broadly into four groups:

(a) In what was expected to be a continuing condition of tight supply and demand, competition for supplies would bid up prices beyond what they would otherwise be, thus hurting everyone, and especially the poorer oil importing countries.

(b) The supply of a basic commodity should not be linked to individual government to government deals because of the risk that an unrelated political dispute would compromise the supply of the commodity. A neutral and efficient supply system, in the form of the companies, was already in existence.

(c) The desire of many oil producing states to purchase arms might cause a dangerous race amongst oil importers to outbid each other in arms supplied for oil.

(d) A common oil policy was a test of the overall strength of European Community solidarity, and agreement between the Community and the United States on this issue was likewise a token of the ability to conclude other and wider Atlantic agreements. Bilateral deals which were not made within a wider framework of agreement thus threatened the overall political unity of the West.

The proponents of bilateral deals tended to take a more pragmatic line, arguing that:

(a) Multilateral agreements between oil importing countries, if achieved, would be interpreted by oil exporters, rightly or wrongly, as a hostile gesture and might therefore provoke confrontation on a much broader front, with consequent dangers to global security.

(b) In the European Community, the basis for co-operative action did not yet exist. In the meantime, nations must act individually, in order both to protect their vital interests and to preserve any possibility of gaining the confidence of the oil producers.

(c) The interests of the United States in the Middle East were not necessarily identical with those of the European Community or its member states. Further, the United States, in contrast with Europe, was able to survive in the future without Middle East oil (and had indeed announced her intention to do so through 'Project Independence'). Bilateral deals could not therefore threaten an accord which did not exist; but, if such deals succeeded in increasing the amount of oil available globally beyond what would otherwise be produced, all would benefit.

Considerable suspicion on the part of the oil producers attended the preparations for the Washington Conference, although it had quickly been announced that the consumers' conference would be followed by a consumer-producer conference. Amongst the consumers, too, the split widened between the French and the other European Community members. Algeria accused the United States of attempting to impose a protectorate on oil consumers and producers, and advocated the holding of a United Nations world commodity conference. Iraq published an open letter to President Nixon making the same suggestion. France, which had also nominated the U.N. as the appropriate discussion body, postponed her decision to attend in Washington until the last moment. Japan made it clear that she saw the conference as only the first step towards what should become a dialogue between oil producing and oil consuming countries. In short, conditions were far from propitious for the success of the Conference.

Dr. Kissinger's opening statement[8] in Washington proposed seven areas for co-operative exploration: energy conservation, alternative energy sources, research and development, energy sharing, international financial co-operation, the situation of less developed countries, and consumer-producer relations. Under the last heading, he argued that the proposed consumer-producer conference would not lead to confrontation, but would form the basis of a new co-operative relationship. But it would do so only if consumers did not seek selfish advantages, either as a group or individually, and only if they had first established a solid foundation of co-operation amongst themselves. He further proposed the establishment of a consumer co-ordinating group to carry forward the work of the consumer conference.

There then followed an attack on all the principles of the Conference by France, and an attempt by the others, particularly the Europeans, to reach a joint compromise line, close to the American position but including the French.

The search for a compromise proved unsuccessful. France, in particular, remained totally opposed to the proposals for a continuing organization to follow up Conference decisions, and in the end refused to accept all or part of four of the major paragraphs in the final communiqué,[9] which dealt with various proposals for future consumer co-operation. The Conference nevertheless resulted in a decision by all but one of the consumer nations to co-operate —despite the original reservations of more than one participant— and, in particular, in an unprecedented agreement by eight members of the European Community to over-ride the firm decision of a ninth and senior member. These results were both worthy of note.

Although another part of the Conference's outcome—an understanding not to prosecute further bilateral oil supply deals remains unwritten—it is abundantly clear that the Washington accord also involved the rejection of bilateralism in its broadest sense. Contacts have admittedly taken place since between Washington signatories and individual oil producers, for example, between Italy and Libya and between Germany and Iran, albeit without any clear result. At the same time, however, groups of consumer country officials have been set up and are already functioning in the areas nominated for joint action .The overall commitment to co-operation seems, in fact, to be viable, despite problems such as U.S. resentment at the European Community's long-postponed decision to open a dialogue with Arab oil producers on broad principles of co-operation.

It is not easy to draw lessons from the Washington Conference on bilateralism versus multilateralism in other resource situations. *Détente* between the United States and the Soviet Union, their tight inter-relationship over a Middle East settlement, the U.S. defence commitment to Europe, the credibility of a U.S. threat to use force to solve Middle East oil supply restrictions, and other super-power considerations are embroiled in the international politics of oil to a totally different degree than is likely to occur with, say, bauxite or copper. This argues both for and against a quicker and less dramatic resolution of future consumer country differences over other resource problems. An optimistic view would stress the learning experience of Washington and its continuing aftermath, in the sense that the difficulties and hard decisions tied up in consumer negotiations on this scale are unlikely in future to be underestimated even for less obviously vital resources. On the other hand, the indications remain strong that the immediate response of a consumer nation faced with a restriction of supply which threatens the smooth running of a high employment economy without raising serious international issues is simply to pay more and thereby obtain the supply, and in the longer term, if possible, to develop alternatives domestically.

Notes

1. Measurements of the degree of self-sufficiency in metals can cause confusion. Conventions have not been standardized. For example, the self-sufficiency of Japan for bauxite is zero but for aluminium is 34 per cent, because of the contribution, in the latter case, of scrap. We have adopted, as a measurement of metals self-sufficiency:—the metal content of indigenous mine production plus indigenous scrap arisings as a percentage of total metal consumption. This reflects the security conveyed to industrial nations by their stocks of metal-in-use, from which scrap supplies arise.

2. Industry forecasts.

3. *Petroleum Intelligence Weekly*, 14 May 1973.

4. *Le Monde*, 4 December 1973.

5. *Financial Times*, 8 January 1974.

6. United States Information Service, *The Times*, 13 December 1973.

7. *The Times*, 17 December 1973.

8. United States Information Service, 12 February 1974.

9. *The Times*, 14 February 1974.

7 The independents

There is a group of nations which resemble each other in little apart from the fact that their resource endowment and general geo-political position insulate them considerably from the process of dependence and adaptation which links the less developed resource exporters and the main resource importers. The group falls naturally into two categories: Australia and Canada; the U.S.S.R. and China. In each case, as would be expected in countries of continental dimensions, there seems to be clear evidence—albeit qualified and conjectural for China—of ample resources to support continued indigenous economic growth and, if necessary, sustain considerable exports to resource deficient countries. But in each case economic growth does not depend wholly on continued resource exports. This dissimilarity to the less developed resource exporters, combined with changing political postures and national objectives, conveys some independence and breadth to the policy options open to these nations.

Australia

With 13 million people in a land mass extending for 3 million square miles and covering vast mineral reserves, with a radically new outlook on Australian national identity, on foreign policy, and economic management, Australia now has the opportunity to take a much more independent rôle in international affairs, and in particular, in the affairs of the Third World.

Australia's rise to prominence as a resource producer has been swift, particularly in recent years, as Table 7.1 illustrates.

The resource reserve endowment on which this pattern of production is based is more difficult to quantify because, apart from all the intrinsic problems of reserve estimation which were described in Chapter 2, there remains an enormous area of territory still to be

Table 7.1. *Australian Resource Production, 1967 and 1972*

	Production (Thousand Tons)		Position in World Producers	
	1967	1972	1967	1972
Iron Ore	16,887	65,000	9	3
Bauxite	4,678	15,910	4	1
Nickel	2	38	8	5
Copper	95	200	11	9
Zinc	347	519	5	3
Coal	58,091	81,000	10	10

Source: *World Bureau of Metal Statistics 1973; Mining Annual Review 1972.*

prospected in detail. In 1938 the Australian Government was concerned at the apparent insufficiency of iron ore reserves, then estimated at 250 million tons, and imposed an export embargo. But
this was before the era of prospecting revealed reserves one hundred
times that amount in the state of Western Australia alone. Similarly,
it was not until the discovery of the Seipa bauxite deposit in 1955
that it could be known that Queensland possesses one-third of
known world reserves of bauxite. It is now scarcely open to doubt
that the continent contains massive reserves of a wide range of
resources, well beyond the medium to long term needs of even a
healthily growing domestic economy. This is not true, however, of
presently known oil reserves, which contain only about fifteen years
supply. Exploration is proceeding at a very high level and prospects
for further discoveries seem good.

Government policy towards the growth and management of
resource industries has been relatively quiescent until recent times.
The investment boom of the 1960s which underwrote the production
figures quoted above was mainly financed by foreign companies.
The proportion of foreign ownership in Australian industry grew
sharply during the 1960s in response to the increasingly attractive
prospects of Australian minerals in world markets and of the
Australian domestic market to foreign based industries. Indeed
investment also took place in response to a vigorous drive by
Australia to attract such investment.

Recent estimates[1] suggest that foreign ownership of Australian
business as a whole has risen from about 20 per cent in 1948/1949
to around 35 per cent in 1970/1. Within the total, some industries
are heavily dominated by overseas ownership, notably automobiles
(95 per cent), pharmaceuticals (81 per cent) and, according to the
Minerals and Energy Minister,[2] mining is 62 per cent foreign
owned.

Political reaction to this situation developed piecemeal. Concern might be expressed on the occasion of specific takeover bids or practices of foreign owned companies which were felt to be inimical to Australian interests, but little concrete action followed and nothing in the way of a fully worked out policy emerged. In 1968, a takeover bid for a life insurance company was vetoed by the Government, and not long afterwards a limit of 15 per cent was set on foreign ownership of a uranium company. From 1971, however, the pace quickened suddenly. The Australian Industrial Development Corporation was established in April 1971, with the objective of promoting industrial development 'whilst maintaining maximum Australian ownership and control'.[3] A Senate Committee was also appointed to look into overseas investment in Australia. Then there took place several attempted takeover bids which seemed to catalyze opinion. One of the best known was that of Thomas Nationwide Transport Industries of Sydney, which attempted to acquire Ansett Transport Industries of Melbourne, an airline operator. The bid was abandoned after protests concerning the (minority) foreign ownership of Thomas acquiring control of Australia's only private enterprise airline.

In December 1972, after an election campaign which gave some prominence to 'buying back' Australia from foreign ownership, a Labour Government was elected under Gough Whitlam. A few weeks later, following a dispute between the Federal Government and the Queensland and New South Wales authorities over the price of coal exports, the Minister for Minerals and Energy, Mr. Connor, announced plans to impose export controls on all minerals. The object was to ensure that Australia received the full market price for mineral exports, and the specific allegations were that Japan was paying $A13·58 per ton for Australian coal against a market price of $A17·39 per ton, and that the terms of iron ore export contracts failed to provide for changes in the value of the U.S. dollar.

This move was followed on 12 April 1973 by a proposal to establish a National Petroleum and Minerals Authority with powers to engage in all facets of the oil business. Introducing his proposals in the House of Representatives, Mr. Connor referred to OPEC's belief that maximization of production of a finite resource might be against the interest of the producing country.[4] The August Budget then removed tax exemption from all profits in gold mining and from 20 per cent of profits from several other minerals, including bauxite, nickel, copper, and uranium. (A regulation had already been made requiring 25 per cent of loans from overseas to be deposited with the Reserve Bank interest-free until the discharge of the loan, but this was widely interpreted not so much as a long-term policy measure to increase Australian domestic investment as a short-term means of halting the flow of 'hot money' which had flowed into Australia during 1972.)

Also in August 1973, a bill was introduced to enhance the standing of the Australian Industry Development Corporation (AIDC). Without providing for any takeover of existing foreign owned operations, it was made clear that the object of the government was to maximize the Australian component of any future development of significance. The scheme envisaged was that a future foreign investor seeking a stake in Australian minerals would be directed towards investment bonds which would be linked to a secure supply of the minerals in question in addition to income and growth in the value of the bond. Control over resource projects would, however, remain in the hands only of the AIDC. Australians would be encouraged to invest in the AIDC through various savings plans incorporating tax concessions. The AIDC was therefore intended to be the major vehicle for capital raising and funding new projects in resource development.

The dedication of the Australian Government to full national control of significant resource developments was made clear in October 1973 when it was revealed that the Woodside-Burmah exploration group had been told by the government that the gas discoveries made by the group off the north-west coast would be acquired at well-head and developed downstream by the government. No price has yet been announced for the acquired reserves. Simultaneously it was announced that the AIDC, together with Ampol Petroleum Company, had acquired a 50 per cent share in two drilling rigs owned by Ocean Drilling and Exploration, a U.S. Company.

Further clarification of government policy was forthcoming during a ministerial meeting in Tokyo, led by the Prime Minister, in late October 1973. In a public address,[5] Mr. Whitlam described the five points upon which Australian mineral resource policy was based:

—to ensure that Australia's own future energy needs and industrial requirements are met.

—to take into full account the effect of developing the traditional lands of the aborigines, where considerable mineral reserves—especially of uranium—had been found.

—to enlarge opportunities for Australians to take a greater share in the ownership and development of the country's mineral wealth.

—to encourage more processing within Australia of minerals indigenously produced.

—to ensure fair prices for Australian production in world markets.

Canada

Canada occupies a singular position on the resources stage. Similar to Australia in the ratio of land mass and resource reserves to population, sharing a colonial past, similar also in her recent more assertive and questioning attitude to her rôle in the international community, she cannot escape the unique implications of the presence on her southern border of the world's richest economy. The options open to Canada in the new circumstances of international dealings in resources will inevitably be coloured by the history and problems of U.S. involvement in her extractive industry.

Canadian mineral production attained a value of $6·4 billion in 1972, accounting for over 6 per cent of GNP. Ranking as the world's leading producer of nickel and zinc, and a leading producer and exporter of iron ore, copper, zinc, lead, and other metals, Canada also has massive reserves of oil, hitherto uneconomic, in the form of tar sands.

Table 7.2. *Canadian Resource Production, 1972*

	Production (*Thousand Tons*)	Position in World Producers
Nickel	265	1
Iron Ore	39,000	5
Copper	801	3
Zinc	1,324	1
Lead	371	4

Source: World Bureau of Metal Statistics 1973; Mining Annual Review 1972.

The cornerstone of Canadian economic development this century has been foreign investment. Before World War I British portfolio investment financed substantial parts of basic sectors of the economy, especially transportation. After that war and ever since, the outstanding component of foreign capital has been direct U.S. investment, the total value of which now stands higher in Canada than in the whole of Europe.

Between 1945 and 1967 the book value of U.S. long-term investment in Canada rose from just under $5 billion to $28 billion, with the direct investment portion increasing from around $2 billion to $17 billion. About half the increase in U.S. direct investment during this period was for the development of natural resources. At the end of 1967 the value of capital employed in oil and natural gas was $9·7 billion. Three-quarters was controlled by non-residents, and of the non-resident controlled proportion, 81 per cent lay with the U.S. residents. Similar figures held for mining and smelting (65 per cent foreign owned; 85 per cent of that by U.S. residents).

Why did foreign investment in resources take place? Firstly, both Federal and Provincial Governments, seeking economic growth, made conscious attempts by tariff or more direct policies to attract resource investment, whether domestic or foreign. Given the scale of capital required in relation to the size of the Canadian capital market, it was inevitable that the bulk should be foreign. The main determinant was, of course, the industrial logic of 'backwards vertical integration' by U.S. based mineral companies. With a pre-existing consumer market and with processing and fabricating facilities set up to serve that market, the natural course was to seek ample and secure supplies of the raw material from a contiguous friendly country offering attractive tax terms and the freedom to obtain really significant scale economies.

Whereas the benefits of this type of investment are clear—the provision of capital, technology, and managerial skills, the opening up of undeveloped regions and a contribution to the national balance of payments—from the Canadian point of view there have also been drawbacks. The very capital intensive nature of resource industries has meant that their employment impact has been small. In 1970 mineral production accounted for over 6 per cent of the Canadian GNP but employed directly only 1·4 per cent of the labour force (although the indirect employment effect would increase the ratio to some degree). Backwards vertical integration has tended to leave the processing industries in the U.S. or other foreign markets—although there are sound economic reasons for this, for example, in petroleum refining. Apart altogether from the economic dis-benefits, which are often difficult to estimate with any precision, great weight must be attached to the constant complaint that large resource investments vertically integrated back to the

U.S. market effectively deprive Canada of autonomy in planning the scale, direction, and priorities of her industrial activity.

The Canadian policy response to foreign investment has paralleled, indeed foreshadowed, that of Australia. In the 1920s and 1930s steps had already been taken to prevent foreign control over railways, airlines, buslines, and radio stations. Similar provisions were extended to life insurance companies and TV stations in the 1950s. The pace of regulatory policy-making increased sharply in the 1960s and 1970s and its coverage become more clearly focused on the manufacturing and extractive sectors. In 1966 appeared the first comprehensive statement of the Canadian Government's view on the 'guiding principles of good corporate behaviour' which should be followed by foreign owned companies.[6]

1. Pursuit of sound growth and full realisation of the company's productive potential, thereby sharing the national objective of full and effective use of the nation's resources.
2. Realisation of maximum competitiveness through the most effective use of the company's own resources, recognising the desirability of progressively achieving appropriate specialisation of productive operations within the internationally affiliated group of companies.
3. Maximum development of market opportunities in other countries as well as in Canada.
4. Where applicable, to extend processing of natural resource products to the extent practicable on an economic basis.
5. Pursuit of a pricing policy designed to assure a fair and reasonable return to the company and to Canada for all goods and services sold abroad, including sales to the parent company and other foreign affiliates.
6. In matters of procurement, to search out and develop economic sources of supply in Canada.
7. To develop as an integral part of the Canadian operation wherever practicable, the technological research and design capability necessary to enable the company to pursue appropriate product development programs so as to take full advantage of market opportunities domestically and abroad.
8. Retention of a sufficient share of earnings to give appropriate financial support to the growth requirements of the Canadian operation, having in mind a fair return to shareholders on capital invested.
9. To work towards a Canadian outlook within management, through purposeful training programs, promotion of qualified Canadian personnel and inclusion of a major proportion of Canadian citizens on its Board of Directors.
10. To have the objective of a financial structure which provides opportunity for equity participation in the Canadian enterprise by the Canadian public.
11. Periodically to publish information on the financial position and operations of the company.

12. To give appropriate attention and support to recognised national objectives and established Government programs designed to further Canada's economic development and to encourage and support Canadian institutions directed toward the intellectual, social and cultural advancement of the community.

In 1970 policy statements were issued on foreign ownership in the Canadian uranium industry. Foreign ownership had to be limited to 33 per cent for companies controlling demonstrated productive capacity. No limit was to be placed on exploration activity. No divestment of existing foreign ownership over 33 per cent was envisaged, but any transfers of ownership where the majority ownership was foreign had to be to Canadians.

In 1972 a Bill was introduced by the Minister of Revenue, Mr. Herb Gray, to subject all foreign takeovers of Canadian firms of a certain minimum size to government approval. This would be forthcoming only if the foreign investor was able to establish that the purchase would result in 'significant benefit' to Canada, defined in terms of increased employment, the effects on existing industry and the effect on 'productivity, industrial efficiency, technological development, product innovation and product variety in Canada'.[7]

It is notable that this measure followed a lengthy study of foreign investment (the Gray Report)[8] which specifically considered the merits of three broad policy approaches: the designation of key sectors of the Canadian economy in which Canadian ownership was to be emphasized; the fixed rules approach, whereby it would be mandatory, for example, that Canadians held a certain proportion of all firms in Canada of economic significance; and the review process approach whereby an administrative mechanism would be set up to examine foreign investment proposals case by case. Observing that the first approach typified policy to date, the report came down in favour of the third alternative basically on the grounds of its flexibility. It could concentrate on that relatively small proportion of foreign investment which was of greatest concern to Canada at any point in time. Acknowledging that the resource sector might appear to be a natural area for a key sector approach the report noted that there was no reason to be confident that Canadian controlled resource companies would undertake any greater degree of processing of raw materials in Canada than a foreign owned company—everything else being equal.

That other things will not remain equal has become evident following two events, the first of which was the establishment in 1971 of the Government-backed Canada Development Corporation

(CDC). Among the specific elements in its general brief to stimulate Canadian industrial development was a clear interest in projects which would process Canadian raw materials before export. To date, the CDC has invested in petrochemicals, pharmaceuticals and, notably, in the diversified U.S. multi-national resource company Texasgulf which is active in Canadian silver and zinc. It has expressed interest also in the oil and gas fields. Secondly, two pieces of linked legislation appeared in 1973 and 1974. A Foreign Investment Review Act was passed in the former year, designed to implement the conclusion of the Gray Report and including in its regulations the requirement for a potential foreign investor, in the case of a resource company, to provide information on the degree of processing to be carried out in Canada. In March 1974 an amendment was tabled to the Export and Import Permits Act whereby the Government may control the export of raw materials. The inference for foreign investors in the resource field seems clear.

The Communist World

Discussion of Soviet and Chinese resource facts and policies is inhibited by the lack of reliable data. Much of the argument has to be based on surmise plus outdated or suspect statistics. Nevertheless some parts of the picture are discernible at least in broad outline. Both countries have in the past deliberately aimed at a policy of self-sufficiency in resources and have generally avoided significant dependency on international markets except where this was unavoidable. There has been, however, extensive Soviet trade with the Council for Mutual Economic Aid (COMECON) states and some with Western Europe. And China, with a rather different industrial history, has had to import quantities of various resources. The Soviet Union has within its vast land area very large proven resource reserves and numerous geological structures indicating a considerable potential fuel and mineral endowment. The same statement cannot be so confidently made about China, but the most recent indications suggest that resource shortages are generally due not to deficient reserves but to problems of exploitation. It is broadly true of both countries that many resource deposits are located in desolated and inhospitable terrain, giving rise to very high extraction and transportation costs, and requiring for their exploitation advanced technology and equipment which is in very short supply in the Communist world. Both countries therefore face choices on the degree to which they will be prepared to open up their internal resource economies with the help of outsiders, and which partners they should choose. They have also to consider how their international political interests might be advanced by action they might take relative to the resource problems of other countries.

The U.S.S.R.

The U.S.S.R. is the leading world producer of coal, iron ore, manganese, chrome, and several other minerals; it comes second to the U.S.A. in crude oil and natural gas output and second to Canada in nickel and zinc production. Reserves as yet untapped hold out the possibility of increasing and sustaining production of a wide range of resources at very high levels. For example coal output of one billion tons by the end of the century has been postulated.[9]

An integral part of the centrally planned Soviet economy is the production of resources for non-domestic use. Fuels, metals, and minerals accounted for over 37 per cent of total official exports during 1972. Most of these went to East European satellite states, for whom the U.S.S.R. is the main raw materials supplier, especially in oil, iron ore, and fertilizers. Outside Eastern Europe, however, there are important Soviet exports of chromite, manganese, and platinum. The two main current exceptions to Soviet self-sufficiency in unprocessed minerals are tin, where about one-fifth of supplies are imported, mainly from Bolivia; and bauxite, where indigenous grades are of poor quality, requiring high grade imports from Hungary, Yugoslavia, Greece, and elsewhere.

In recent years, Soviet acceptance of the need to acquire Western technological skills to develop her indigenous resources has become more pronounced, though negotiations to translate intentions into reality have usually been protracted and sometimes abortive. Such negotiations have often been conducted simultaneously with offers on the part of the U.S.S.R. to give equipment and technical assistance in the same fields to less developed countries. For example, Japanese and European companies have been in discussions to assist the development of Soviet copper and nickel when similar schemes were being proposed by the U.S.S.R. for her to assist Chile and Cuba. Most notably perhaps, a wide range of advanced Western steelmaking and finishing technology is being imported at a time when iron and steel plant construction accounts for about one-fifth of Soviet economic and technical assistance to Communist and developing nations.

It is in the oil and natural gas sector that the Soviet Union meshes most conspicuously with the international system. Soviet oil exports to the West have been running recently at around 47 million tons per year. Supply contracts for natural gas have been agreed with France, Austria, Germany, and Italy, usually under a barter arrangement in return for steel pipe and gas industry equipment. Agreement in principle—though not on terms—has been reached with U.S. and Japanese companies for vast projects involving Siberian natural gas developments in various locations, notably Yakutsk in Eastern Siberia, involving a 2,000 mile pipeline to Nakhodka on the Pacific, and in Tyumen in Western Siberia, involving a pipeline of 1,500 miles to Murmansk on the Barents Sea. Similar projects for oil exports have not progressed smoothly. A tentative scheme for developing Tyumen oil reserves for export mainly to Japan via pipeline or a more recently mooted railway suffered a reverse when the original export target to Japan of 40 million tons per year was revised by the U.S.S.R. to 25 million tons per year. However, it seems clear that expansion of the Soviet oil industry depends on the opening up of Siberian deposits. The old oil producing centres in the Caucasus and around the Caspian are at their peak or in decline. The signs are that the U.S.S.R. has accepted in principle the necessity of acquiring Western technology and credits for the enormous exploitation projects required. Before such schemes can come to fruition in the late 1980s, it seems likely that Soviet assessments of domestic and East European oil requirements, when set against likely interim supplies, will allow only a restricted and rapidly declining margin for crude oil sales to the West, however desirable such sales are for hard currency earnings. This situation seems to obtain despite the encouragement given by the U.S.S.R to her East European dependencies for them to arrange for part of their oil requirements to be met by direct supply deals with oil exporting countries, notably Iraq.

The Middle East war and the OPEC price rises have put many Soviet policies to the test. As far as external political relations are concerned, the commitment to *détente* with the U.S.A. has apparently proved stronger than the temptation—or perhaps more accurately, the ability—to maximize diplomatic gains in the Middle East, although both Soviet and U.S. intentions have been far from clear. In the case of Soviet crude oil supplies to the West, it appears that no time was lost in revising prices upwards to equate with the levels set by OPEC, and this applied even to very old customers

such as Finland, which obtains the bulk of its oil supplies from the
U.S.S.R., and the West German company VEBA which has been a
purchaser for 16 years. The OPEC price rises thus had the effect
of enabling the U.S.S.R. to maintain or even increase her hard currency earnings targets from crude oil sales despite the likelihood of
lowered availability of volumes for export. Soviet oil supply contracts with East Europe have fixed prices until the end of 1975, but
negotiations for contract renewals commenced in 1974. It seems
likely that prices will be increased and volumes will be limited. The
economic leverage accruing to the U.S.S.R. from its control of
around 85 per cent of East European oil supplies may be weakened
to the extent that a further impetus is given to supply deals between
individual COMECON and OPEC countries, but there seems
little doubt that the bulk of supplies will continue to come under
Soviet control.

China

Facts on Chinese resource operations and policies are scant. The
publication of official statistics has been virtually non-existent since
1960. In recent years, following her admission into the United
Nations in 1971 and the contacts prior and subsequent to the visits
of President Nixon and Prime Minister Tanaka, the position has
improved somewhat. The broad picture emerging is of a huge nation
of possibly 800 million people, not easily classifiable, still in many
ways a developing country, and pursuing its own very individual
and self-reliant path towards industrialization and agricultural
modernization—'walking on two legs'. The aim of Chinese economic
policy is to balance the development of both the modern and the
traditional sectors under conditions which encourage the full contribution of indigenous technology and resources and minimize
dependence on outside powers. In the various stages of Chinese
development this balance between the sectors has tended to vary in
sympathy with the oscillation between a centralized and a decentralized mode of economic conduct, the former favouring the
build-up of the modern sector, with large-scale resource projects,
and the latter putting a greater focus on the traditional sector and
on small-scale and regional resource developments. In the coal
industry, for example, the first type of policy would aid the expansion
and modernization of the top twelve coal combines which are
controlled by the Ministry of Fuel and Chemical Industry and

which together produced around one-third of China's 1972 estimated output of 400 million tons. The decentralized policy, most recently articulated during the Cultural Revolution of 1966–70, would call for greater reliance on the thousands of small- and medium-sized mines scattered around the country under the control of individual communes, many producing from 100 to 1,000 tons per day under traditional highly labour intensive methods, which accounted for most of the rest of national output.

China is the world's third largest coal producer, after the U.S.A. and the U.S.S.R., and coal accounts for around 85 per cent of her energy requirements.[10] The oil industry, which was estimated to have produced around 30 million tons of crude in 1972 or not much more than 1 per cent of world output, is relatively undeveloped, but capable of meeting current domestic needs. However, it was reported in January 1974[11] that the Chinese Premier, Chou En-lai, had told the Japanese Foreign Minister that Chinese crude production had reached 50 million tons per year. Indeed the indications are that crude output is running ahead of refining capacity and giving rise to some small sales of crude, notably to Japan. With production of iron ore running at around 50 million tons, China is prominent amongst world producers and is self-sufficient, but there are severe deficits in steel making and finishing technology and in advanced steel products. It seems to be increasingly acceptable for these deficits to be satisfied by imports, mainly from Japan. China is dependent on imports for roughly half her consumption of aluminium, copper, lead, and zinc, and for almost all her nickel. For all except the last named, the problem is apparently not the absolute lack of reserves but the poor quality of the known ores and, above all, the absence of mining technology and equipment. The main sources for non-ferrous metal imports seem to be settling down as Chile, Peru, and Zambia for copper, Peru and Canada for lead and zinc, and Canada for nickel. Medium-term trade agreements have been signed with Chile and Peru, while China is building a 1,000 mile railway linking the Zambian copper belt with the Tanzanian port of Dar-es-Salaam, involving 15,000 Chinese technicians.[12] In April 1974 it was reported that China had also agreed to provide an interest-free loan of about £31 million to develop Tanzanian coal and iron ore mines and link them to the railway.

Chinese mineral exports have had a spasmodic history; they are currently restricted to relatively small quantities of tin, tungsten, fluorspar, and antimony. The straightforward interpretation of

Chinese policy in these markets is that her interest increases in line with the market price.

It is not possible to predict the future course of Chinese resource policy with any confidence. Amongst other things, the present leadership is ageing, and it is not known for certain what emphasis the likely new leaders will place on self-reliance or the philosophy of 'walking on two legs'. The balance of probabilities would indicate that the pace of industrialization will increase and that the natural complementarity of the Chinese and Japanese economies will be exploited, partly for fear of Soviet-Japanese alliances as much as for the intrinsic economic benefits. It has been made clear, for example, that China is unhappy about the proposed joint ventures to exploit and transport Tyumen crude by pipeline or railway to the Pacific, since either would run very close to the Chinese border. Whatever the composition of the next Chinese administration, it seems likely that there will be a higher proportion of technocrats to revolutionary leaders than heretofore, and that the planners will have a greater freedom to enter international trade in order to fill the gaps they have identified in Chinese technological capability. If this emphasis is to be associated with centralism and the modern sector there seems every possibility that the oil and electrical sectors will receive priority, and with them the associated requirements for steel, copper, and advanced equipment, all of which can be developed rapidly only with imported Western technology.

An Independent Resource Policy

Despite the Procrustean flavour of the rubric which associates four such disparate nations as Australia, Canada, the U.S.S.R. and China, they all have in common a degree of insulation from the 'main line' resource exporter/importer relationships.[13] Not being directly involved in these processes of shifting power and dependency, the nations we have termed 'independents' have some flexibility of choice as to what posture in the resource arena best suits their political and economic objectives. A simple model of the policy options theoretically open to them would have three main components:

(a) to take profits: as OPEC policies increase the price and scarcity of crude oil, and if and when other resource producers are able to do likewise, the value of Siberian, Canadian, and other deposits rises accordingly. One strategy is to realize the asset;

(b) to obtain political or strategic advancement: during the period of consumer country dependence on OPEC oil or CIPEC copper it would be open to the independents to exploit the situation to their political advantage, for example, China or the U.S.S.R. in the Middle East or Africa;

(c) to opt out: a plausible assumption holds that resources surplus to domestic requirements in independent countries will be drawn inexorably into the international market by the price mechanism. But it is conceivable that a swing to the self-reliant, traditional sector approach in Chinese policies or a hardening of Australian or Canadian economic nationalism could result in more conservationist and isolationist policies.

While these options as presented have the appearance of stark alternatives, the reality is more likely to be that of some mixture of the three. It will be some time before the policies of the independents mesh sufficiently with the international system to enable an adequate analysis to be carried out, but of their great potential influence there can be little doubt. From the material so far available it is clear that despite ideological differences, all independents are prepared to admit option (a) into their policy repertoire. The next test will be to see the influence—or lack of it—exerted by the independents, especially Australia, on the formation and policies of Third World resource producer organizations.

Notes

1. Australian Trade Department Survey and an Australian Treasury economic paper, quoted in *Financial Times*, 28 September 1973.
2. *Financial Times*, 12 October 1973.
3. *Guardian*, 28 September 1973.
4. *Financial Times*, 13 April 1973.
5. Speech quoted in *Oilgram News Service*, 31 October 1973.
6. Letter from Mr Robert Winter, Canadian Minister of Trade, to heads of affiliates of foreign companies, 31 March 1966.
7. *Statement to the [Canadian] House of Commons* by the Honourable Herbert Gray, May 1972.
8. *Direct Investment in Canada*, Information Canada, Ottawa, 1972.
9. *Mining Annual Review*, 1973.
10. *Financial Times*, 17 July 1973.
11. *Financial Times*, 8 January 1974.
12. *Guardian*, 1 April 1974.
13. The list could, of course, be extended. South Africa is another candidate. The aim has been to illustrate rather than enumerate.

8 The poor

The final actor on the resource stage plays a rôle defined almost completely by the actions of the other participants. The greater part of the Southern hemisphere, containing the majority of humanity, consists of countries with low *per capita* incomes, consuming fuel and mineral resources but not, for the most part, producing any in significant quantities. Already hard pressed to survive and grow, what further problems are presented and what options are open to the less developed resource importers in the situation we have been describing?

One of the conceits of commentators based in the rich nations is to lump all developing countries together. The problems and options facing Asian, African, or South American policy makers will be as different as their size, population, social system, and geopolitical position. But generalizations are possible; and many of the broader issues have been thrown into sharp focus by the simultaneously shared experience of oil supply and price difficulties in the developing world following October 1973.

India's Oil Problem

The constraints placed on India's development strategy by OPEC's success in raising the world price of oil provide a detailed illustration of the limited freedom of action open to many Third World countries. It should be remembered, however, that India is relatively rich in mineral resources, unlike many less developed countries (LDCs), although much of this resource endowment remains to be exploited.

As for many poor countries, Indian oil consumption has been increasing rapidly, from 3·3 million tons in 1950 to 22·6 million tons in 1972. Indigenous oil was not discovered until the 1960s and in 1972 crude production was 7·4 million tons, roughly one-third of oil consumption. Recently there has been an encouraging oil find in the offshore Bombay High region; but this was the first commercial oilfield to be found in almost a decade. There are, on the other hand, significant proved reserves of coal, but these are for the most part inaccessibly located. The foreign exchange costs of oil imports have grown rapidly, from a value of R.581 million in 1950 to R.1,940 million in 1971/72, or a little under 11 per cent of the total import bill in the latter year.

In 1971/72 two categories of imports loomed larger than oil—iron and steel at 13 per cent, and machinery at 20 per cent, but a large part of the machinery and some of the steel came under aid or under rupee payments, whereas most of the oil had to be paid for in convertible currency.

The bulk of oil consumption takes place in essential end-use sectors: for example, besides basic industrial uses, consumption arises in trucks and buses, which are the main form of public and goods transport; as an illuminant in the villages which house most of India's 590 million population, and 80 per cent of which have no electricity; as a feedstock for fertilizer production and a power source for irrigation schemes, both essential for food production in a country where diets are meagre.

In the latter half of 1973, final drafts were being produced of India's Fifth Five-Year Plan, which aimed at the removal of poverty and the attainment of self-reliance. Bearing in mind the 60 per cent rise in oil import prices during 1971 and 1972, the planners felt it only prudent to allow for a rise in the price of crude oil to between $4 and $5 per barrel towards the end of the decade. That assumption indicated that non-oil imports would be constrained to a 2 per cent per annum increase if exports grew at 7 per cent per annum, or a 5 per cent increase if exports grew at 10 per cent per annum. In view of the essential nature of Indian non-oil imports, especially those linked to food production, it was difficult to conceive their being restricted to 2 per cent. Even with $4 per barrel oil imports being postulated, therefore, the possibility existed that the entire Indian economic development programme might have to be re-ordered at a lower level to achieve a viable balance of payments position. In the event, the last quarter of 1973 brought about crude prices in excess of $8 per barrel. What options has this totally un-expected economic blow left in the hands of Indian policy makers?

Considering first the courses of action available by the internal restructuring of the Indian economy, there are three possible measures.

(a) *Produce more domestic oil*

The search for oil in India has been generally unrewarding; some relatively small discoveries have been made in Assam and Gujarat, but the best prospects seem to be offshore, near Bombay. Here, as elsewhere, Indian attitudes to foreign investment are being put to the test. Indian policy is to reduce dependence on Western oil companies, and large parts of the industry from exploration to refining have been allocated to the public sector. The Oil and Natural Gas Commission has made successful discoveries, but even before the end-1973 crude price rises, it seemed necessary for non-Indian help to be sought to bridge the growing gap between demand and indigenous supply. Soviet assistance was sought and received following the rejection of exploration proposals by Western companies after years of negotiations. In the re-appraisal following the OPEC price increases, Western companies have returned to conduct exploration. These delays, when added to the inevitably slow process of converting exploratory drillings into commercial production, mean that this course of action will be unable to respond to the short and medium term problems of India's oil supplies.

One side-effect of the increased emphasis on domestic oil prospects has been to highlight a long-standing though previously quiescent territorial dispute between India and her smaller neighbour Sri Lanka. The bone of contention is the tiny uninhabited island of Kachchation, off the North West coast of Sri Lanka. In April 1973 Mrs. Gandhi, the Indian Prime Minister, was reported[1] as dismissing Kachchation as a barren rock of no strategic value. However, only months later reports came in that oil had been discovered on the island, which immediately changed its status in India-Sri Lanka relations.

(b) *Utilize alternative energy sources*

Leaving aside possible nuclear energy developments, the only alternative fuel known to exist in significant quantities in India is coal—perhaps 120 billion tons.

Before the oil price rises, production was scheduled to increase from 80 million tons per year to an ambitious target of 140 million tons at the end of the Fifth Plan, and since the bulk of coal production is remote from the Southern and Western centres of consumption, this output objective was ambitious also in terms of the

implied expansion of the rail transport system. It is therefore difficult
to postulate a massive increase over current targets in the time
span concerned, especially when it seems likely that the coal industry will be undergoing world-wide expansion with consequent
pressure on supplies of coal working machinery. In any case,
a further expansion of coal production would not contribute to
those sectors of the economy requiring liquid fuel—transport,
village illumination, irrigation. Coal consumption might be increased in the railways themselves, but the logistic problems of
maintaining a bigger coal supply network are considerable, and
although the recent policy decision to phase out steam locomotives
in favour of diesel or electric might be reversed or recast, it is
unlikely that new coal burning locomotives could be introduced,
either quickly or easily. Over 90 per cent of installed electricity
generating capacity is already coal fired, limiting significant expansion there. Therefore the industrial sector is the only possible area
for coal to replace oil, and even within industry there will be certain
applications where heat is an essential part of the production process
and where the production technology will call specifically for oil
firing.

Research is currently being directed towards improving the efficiency of some of the most ancient indigenous fuels. For example,
a project studying the generation of methane from cow dung is
under way at the Institute of Economic Research in Kerala, under
the direction of Professor K. N. Raj. Experiments to date suggest it
could be feasible to produce enough 'indigenous' gas in the average
village household to provide some electric light and most of the
cooking fuel requirements, while continuing to use the dung residue
as a fertilizer. This removes the mutual exclusivity of burning dung
for fuel versus using it as fertilizer. The viability of such schemes is
yet to be demonstrated, and in any event would not contribute
greatly outside the rural-traditional sector. Indirectly, of course,
any relief of the pressure on oil requirements would benefit other
sectors such as industry.

(c) *Reduce demand in oil consuming sectors*

In the economy of a poor country like India, the scope for reducing
oil consumption is much more limited than in the industrial nations,
simply because extravagance has never developed. Most of India's
consumption of oil is vital; reduce its use and the production of
food or some other essential commodity is reduced. In the wake

of the October 1973 crude price increase, the Indian Government was forced to raise the retail prices of oil products. It chose to do so selectively by imposing the highest increase (65 per cent) on motor gasoline, thus squeezing the consumption of the private motorist hardest; a smaller rise in the price of kerosene, thus discouraging the move away from wood, coke, and charcoal as a cooking fuel; and no increase in the price of naphtha, which is needed for fertilizer production. The scope for real savings in oil consumption in India, whether by price or volume rationing is exceedingly limited. If agriculture, industry, or transport are denied supplies the economy will wither.

It therefore seems clear that internal adaptation of the Indian energy economy offers little possibility in the current decade of escaping the need to import and somehow to pay for considerable volumes of oil. If India has to pay the world market price for these imports then the effects on her balance of payments would be catastrophic. In 1974/75, assuming an average price of $10 per barrel landed in India, the import bill would be about $1·5 billion, nearly 12 billion rupees, in a year when total export earnings are projected at about 21·5 billion rupees. Of the latter, around one-fifth is in rupee trade with Eastern Europe; therefore oil imports seem destined to account for about three-quarters of India's hard currency earnings.

In this situation, many Indian objectives now seem unattainable, at least for the foreseeable future, and in particular the desire to be self-reliant, which received prominence in the Five Year Plan, must now be frustrated as India turns for further assistance to the outside world. On the basis of the above calculations, the *increase* in oil import costs in 1974/75 would equal or exceed the total of annual aid payments received by India in recent years. The objective of *reducing* reliance on aid within the conventional time span of national planning must now seem totally unrealistic. Nor has the other main objective of the Fifth Five-Year Plan—the abolition of poverty—gone unscathed. The emphasis has already been changed in an attempt to preserve the viability of key industries, the so-called 'core' sector of steel, oil refining, power generation and fertilizers.

After some initial confusion, India was exempted from the Arab oil embargo, as were all those developing countries—the majority— who signalled their support of the Arab side in the Arab-Israeli war. Despite many requests, in which India has frequently taken the lead, OPEC has been unwilling to adopt a two-tier crude pricing system whereby developing countries would be charged a concessionary price, and the industrial nations the full price. (It has however been reported[2] that Iran and Iraq have separately agreed to sell in total some 5 million tons of crude to India during 1974 on deferred terms. The Iranian deal was linked to the supply by India of certain commodities required by Iran—cement, steel, and aluminium, whereas the Iraq deal seems to be a more straightforward crude sale).

Nor has any immediate relief of oil supply problems come from the Indo-Soviet economic agreement which was signed in November 1973. The Trade Protocol for 1974 does not include crude supplies (though one million tons of kerosene are included), and it has been reported that a direct request by India for crude was refused by the U.S.S.R. on the grounds that none was available. On the other hand agreements have been undertaken in the energy sector whereby the U.S.S.R. will assist with drilling rigs and technicians in exploration and production projects for land and offshore crude developments, as well as oil refining and coal mining. Together with assistance to develop the steel, transport, pharmaceutical, and other industries, Soviet aid could amount to the equivalent of 100 billion rupees over the 15-year period of the Agreement on Economic Co-operation. The implications for Indian political independence of such a broadly-based Soviet aid programme, while not insignificant, are perhaps less powerful than would be the case if an offer of attractively-priced short and medium term crude supplies were involved. This situation may yet arise.

Third World Choices

The Indian experience with restricted oil supplies and increased oil prices is not unique. The whole of the developing world has been likewise affected, and more severely affected than the industrial world. This uneven incidence of advantage would be repeated if similar conditions prevailed for other resources, although probably the supply and price of oil is the most crucial. Both OPEC itself and individual OPEC members—notably Iran and Venezuela—have called for the creation of OPEC-backed funds to help finance the oil imports of LDCs. One of the first concrete proposals to emerge was that of the Shah of Iran, which envisaged a fund contributed to by both OPEC and the industrialized nations, staffed by the World Bank and the IMF. The Iranian Government has pledged financial support, believed to be around $150 million, for a fund whose total size would be between $2 billion and $3 billion per annum. It was reported on 8 April 1974,[3] that an OPEC Conference had decided, subject to ratification, to set up a similar fund based on voluntary subscriptions of OPEC members and administered by OPEC. It would provide LDCs with soft loans over 25 years. Separately, Arab oil producers have responded to the requests of the 42 member Organisation of African Unity, most of whom supported the Arab side in the war, by agreeing to set up an Arab Bank for African Development with funds of around $200 million. But supply and price are only two aspects of the issue as it impacts on resource deficient LDCs (RDLDCs). The resource issue is only one part of the complex of development problems and objectives facing the Third World.

There is diversity amongst these least well favoured countries which points away from any single solution to their problems. For example, there are few developing countries which are *totally* lacking in significant deposits of any non-agricultural resource; but there are probably some. Not all developing countries are without a significant indigenous community of scientists and managers; but most are. Some of these nations are politically important to the major powers, as is India. Some have potential geographical advantages in the resource business, for example, a situation on the major sea routes. These distinctions are important, but there are too many of them for systematic treatment here. Instead, we will touch upon two resource issues other than supply and price— exploration and research—and hint at the pattern of similarities and differences in the choices open to the resource deficient Third World.

Exploration

The distinction between absolute and relative poverty of resource endowment is crucial. (One strategically placed oil field or coal deposit could make all the difference—albeit in a ten year span.) Therefore it is obviously important for the resource deficient LDCs to encourage comprehensive exploration activities. The object will be to identify not only high-grade large volume deposits suitable for export but also smaller and less pure deposits which might be important for the build up of industrial sites throughout the country, especially when the transportation system is rudimentary. (Local industry in China has frequently depended on small and impure deposits of coal and minerals.) Resource deficient LDCs may invite foreign companies to explore or may establish a state company to do so, seeking funds from the United Nations or via bilateral assistance. The main issues arising are the skills necessary to conduct the survey, its financing, and the terms under which exploration effort is obtainable.

There seems little doubt that for those countries whose apparent deposits are least, whose financial and technical resources are slight and whose territories are large, the foreign companies offer the only really practical means of meeting their needs. It is not simply a question of finance. United Nations and World Bank grants may be available, although this usually means less money is available for other development activities. The outstanding contribution of the foreign companies is a reservoir of scarce skills, both technical and managerial, by the use of which surveys can be carried out efficiently and quickly. It has been estimated that 55 per cent of the land area of India has not even been mapped on an adequate geological scale. That proportion would no doubt be even higher in other resource deficient LDCs. A comprehensive exploration programme is therefore an inevitably lengthy undertaking, whose duration can only be minimized by the most efficient and modern techniques. Although some of the basic exploration skills could be brought together and used relatively efficiently even by the worst situated RDLDCs, for example, by establishing regional exploration companies between several developing nations as has been done in West Africa, this would be unlikely to produce quick results. *A fortiori* it would delay the vital revenue earning exploitation stage. For those RDLDCs who are relatively better placed, both in terms of overall 'prosperity', known mineral deposits and the presence of a local technical capability, it will be more attractive to make the attempt to 'go it alone' or at any rate with the maximum possible self-reliance. However, it should be stressed that the ability to contemplate this course of action as a practical proposition will be restricted to those countries at the most advanced end of the RDLDC spectrum.

One of the most interesting schemes for mutual assistance between resource deficient LDCs has been the U.N. proposal of a revolving fund for resource exploration. This envisaged contributions by LDCs on whose territories U.N. exploration projects had found resources. This fund would then finance further exploration projects in other LDCs.

Research and Development

RDLDCs will engage with the issue of research and development in two ways; one increasingly common to all LDCs—self-reliance— and one of special relevance to resource deficit areas—substitution.

China has pursued a policy of self-reliance or technological independence ever since the Soviet Union withdrew its aid in the late 1950s. India is now endeavouring to follow this policy. The Andean Pact and much of Latin America are following suit and the idea now permeates much of U.N. literature on development. As applied to the resource industries the concept revolves around a descriptive 'model' of the behaviour of foreign companies to the effect that technology, management, and capital are shipped over in a package from a parent company to its subsidiary in the LDC. The choice of technology is made by the parent. There is little 'learning effect' for the nationals of the host country. Little consideration is given to the compatibility of the technology with the development objectives of the LDC, especially those concerned with employment. In contrast, self-reliance implies an ability to 'unbundle the technology package' so that nationals of the LDC can pick and choose those elements most appropriate to national needs and can assemble the elements themselves. This clearly implies the generation of a technical and management capability far in excess of what generally exists. The concept does not absolutely exclude packaged transfers of technology. But it denotes the freedom and competence to assess the economic and social costs and benefits of alternative routes of technology acquisition and to take such acquisition decisions in harmony with the development goals of the country. If the packaged transfer is the best it may be chosen. The implications of the full application of self-reliance as described to foreign investment are a weakening of the parent/subsidiary company links and a greater emphasis on technology licensing and LDC direct purchasing of machinery.

Resource deficient LDCs have a special position in the debate about resource substitution technology because those LDCs which thorough exploration proves to have no commercially exploitable reserves are currently in the position awaiting many other areas in the future when deposits become exhausted. Industrialized countries are planning research programmes to find or develop substitute energy and mineral resources against a time-table determined by their industrial capital structure. The resource deficient LDCs have no comparable investment in existing industries; if the capital and technology were available they could contemplate the option of entering immediately into the techniques which will be increasingly common in the rest of the world in the twenty-first century. But it is clear that to 'jump a stage' in the resource utilization sequence would require financial, technical, and manpower requirements beyond the capabilities of most LDCs. The question arising is really whether international effort could be deployed to assist the resource deficient LDCs by using them as laboratories for future world resource technology.

At the present time relatively small amounts of money are spent on research and development specifically for developing countries. It has been estimated that 98 per cent of total world expenditures on research and development take place in the industrialized countries. Of this only less than 1 per cent is devoted to research specifically to solve the problems of the developing world. Nor does the United Nations allocate much for research and development. Only 1 per cent of the United Nations Development Programme (UNDP) budget can be allocated for so-called global projects for research. In 1972 this amounted to less than 2 million dollars per year.

The United Nations Advisory Committee on the Application of Science and Technology to Development has, however, advocated a redistribution of world research and development effort towards objectives more relevant to the needs of developing countries. It has suggested that by the end of the second development decade the governments of the developing countries themselves should allocate a greater percentage of their GNP to their own indigenous scientific and technical capabilities. Further, as a part of the aid programme, the developed countries should transfer funds to support the developing countries' own research and at the same time should allocate approximately 10 per cent of their own research and development resources for work of specific relevance to developing countries.

These proposals were debated in 1973 at the U.N. Intergovernmental Committee on Science and Technology and although the developed country governments did not commit themselves to specific targets, they seemed prepared to move in this direction provided good projects could be identified. The Canadian Government *has* already committed itself to spend 5 per cent of its aid budget on research and development for developing countries and most of this is to support research in the developing countries themselves. In 1971 the Canadian Government established the International Development Research Centre and it is planned that by 1976 this Centre will be spending 40 million dollars a year in support of research for the developing nations.

The absorptive capacity of LDCs for research funds is limited. If relatively large sums of money were to be made available by the rich countries for research into the specific problems of developing countries, it would still be necessary for most of it to be spent in the developed countries simply because this is where most scientists live, and where the most advanced laboratories exist.

This reinforces the major criticism which is levelled against the proponents of LDC self-reliance in technology. Effective technology transfer, it is objected, requires the orchestration of a wide range of scientific skills and this in turn implies a versatile and experienced ability reservoir which is not only absent from most LDCs but can only grow there from the input of expertise by foreign investors.

Furthermore, the acquisition by an LDC of all the elements in its desired technology package would result in the commitment of large sums of very scarce capital. On the other hand the willingness of an LDC to pay a high price in order to increase self-reliance should not be underestimated. The scale of values articulated in such decisions will not necessarily conform to the economic and technical logic as perceived by the industrial nations. And it must be stressed again that a middle class and a fairly sophisticated level of economic and political development does exist in some few resource deficient LDCs like India and Argentina. Here the scientific and technical community and government policy makers are in a position to take decisions on the acquisition of technology. India has consciously devoted large amounts of capital to the development of nuclear energy in order to avoid having to take the whole package from abroad. On the other hand, she has accepted a complete package for a steel plant. Similarly one of the principal criteria which was used in Argentina's award of a contract to build a nuclear power station was the willingness of the tendering foreign contractors to unscramble the package and provide an opportunity for some Argentinian technical inputs. For the majority of resource deficient LDCs, however, the benefits of research seem likely to accrue through three routes: (a) foreign investors, usually multi-national corporations, most of which nowadays provide technical training schemes as part of their operation, thus contributing to the rapid build up of an indigenous cadre of technically competent manpower;

(b) regional associations of RDLDCs pooling their assets and skills in some commonly required aim such as the development of small-scale indigenous energy supplies; or (c) assistance under U.N. or governmental technical assistance programmes. There is no reason why these categories should not overlap. Indeed for the worst hit resource deficient LDCs, especially as concerns fuel supplies, concerted international effort would seem to be essential on the technical as well as the financial front to meet the multiple problem of surviving particular resource deficits, building up a basis for substitutes, and attacking the underlying problem of economic growth.

Generalizing now against the background of the whole range of resource issues facing the resource deficient LDCs, it is difficult to be optimistic about the future for these nations. In particular, there seems to be a real danger that they will become doubly frustrated; not only because of their slow progress towards development and autonomy but because of their inability to emulate even the methods, far less the achievements of their fellow LDCs whose fortunes have been changed through the accidents of their geology. It will be a major test of the existence of Third World solidarity whether the OPEC proposals for aiding oil-importing LDCs bear fruit. But the inescapable conclusion is that only through concerted action by resource rich LDCs and the industrial nations, in a framework which respects the desire for autonomy of the poorest nations, will a solution be forthcoming which approaches the scale of the problem.

Notes

1. *Financial Times*, 23 January 1974.
2. *Guardian*, 22 February 1974; *Petroleum Intelligence Weekly*, 8 April 1974.
3. Report of OPEC Conference, Geneva, 7 April 1974, in *The Times*, 8 April 1974.

9 Implications for policy

By now it will be clear that the resources drama is being played on a very wide stage indeed, and with the number and variety of the cast matched by a whole series of sub-plots. In the best type of detective story the reader is given all the clues but still fails to spot the culprit. In the dénouement, the evidence is skilfully disentangled to prove finally that one person, and only one person, can possibly be the guilty party. In the story of resources, however, that satisfaction will be denied the reader. For one thing, the action has really only begun. The most that can be done at this juncture is to expose one false lead and provide some hints as to how the various actors might interpret their rôles.

One conclusion, above all, seems to us important to restate. The resource challenge confronting the international community is not the problem of halting consumption in the face of a fixed and diminished resource inventory. We have argued, instead, that natural resources have a fluid and ever-changing nature and that grounds exist for optimism—albeit qualified—that technology will solve problems of exploration, extraction, substitution, and environmental impact.

Nor does the crucial case of energy, and, in particular, of oil, countermand this thesis. In the longer-term future, by which is meant beyond 1980, there are sufficient reserves of fuels to cope with probable levels of energy demand: a demand which may be expected to be less prodigal than in the last few decades. In the medium term, up to 1980 or thereabouts, there are opportunities for economizing in oil consumption as well as for the rapid expansion of coal output and the production of relatively small, but useful, quantities of 'unconventional' oil. But, in saying that the energy problem is manageable, we are also saying that it must indeed be managed. It seems essential that, in the medium term, these opportunities for restraining fuel consumption and increasing production should not be missed, if the non-Communist world is not to rely for its balance of energy supplies on countries lacking a strong economic incentive to increase their oil production. With the longer-term future in mind, it is no less essential that investment decisions for the development of new fuels should be taken *also in the short and medium term*, given the long lead-times for such projects. There is a transitional period available for adaptation, stretching from the present day until the end of the decade, and probably somewhat beyond. In this period, the expansion of oil production in those areas where that is possible must be joined by the rapid development of other fuels and the various steps necessary to implement energy economies. These pressing and simultaneous changes will impose—politics apart—a considerable burden on the private and governmental capability for technical and economic decision-making and project management. Most of this burden will be concentrated in the remaining years of the current decade, and on the people and institutions which, for better or worse, are then available to carry it.

In reality, politics will not, of course, be kept apart from such a vital adaptive process. Middle East politics have, obviously, accentuated and hastened the process in the case of oil. Domestic politics in the oil-importing countries will also be engaged, as will international politics amongst those countries and between importers and exporters. As far as domestic politics are concerned, we have argued that a suddenly increased price for a substantially and widely-used import cannot easily be accommodated by modern economic systems in a smooth and costless 'textbook' manner. This suggests that inflationary pressures are likely to be enhanced in the industrial countries, with all the attendant problems of maintaining equity between different sections of society. International equity will present no less urgent problems, for reasons which include the differential international impact of inflation but which also involve, much more dramatically, all the considerations of super-power interest and European unity which were discussed in Chapter 6. Within the limits set by politics, we believe that there does exist a 'managerial' solution to the problem of adapting to a new pattern of fuel consumption and production. We have also argued that the balance of payments effects of higher oil prices on industrialized economies are themselves manageable.

Unfortunately, there is no guarantee that the necessary steps will be taken in time to deal with either the forecast shortfall in supply or the balance of payments effects of sufficient but expensive oil supplies. In this connection, the balance of payments problems present the more immediate hazards, if only because countries cannot postpone the settlement of import deficits until the IMF or some other international agency has accumulated sufficient special funds to meet their new borrowing requirements. If, as a result, deficits have to be financed on commercial terms, countries may soon exhaust their credit-worthiness and be obliged to impose controls on imports or to take drastic deflationary measures, thus distorting both trade and economic development.

The terms of the possible 'managerial' solution which we have envisaged would not exclude the natural operation of market forces e.g. through consumer response to higher energy prices, but they do point very clearly away from the *unaided* operation of market forces. Time periods, often approaching and sometimes exceeding ten years from the date of a decision, are required to bring into operation major new energy production projects, such as new oil fields, coal mines or nuclear power stations. Long lead-times (as well as complex problems of synchronized planning) are also associated with the complementary investments often required in the context of major energy extraction projects, as in the cases of rail transportation facilities for new coal mines or drilling rigs for new oil developments. Re-tooling for smaller cars and up-rating insulation standards in house construction are parallel examples of changes in the technology of energy consumption which require time for implementation and adjustment. In Chapter 4, moreover, we discussed the phenomenon, in complex industrial economies, of a very heavy commitment to particular patterns of raw material supply. Investment decisions throughout non-Communist economies are also generally taken in a decentralized fashion. In these circumstances, when oil prices move in the rapid and discontinuous way we have experienced recently, it seems highly unlikely that unaided market forces will be able to generate the required direct and complementary energy investments at the time they are needed. An urgent necessity for industrial oil-importing countries is therefore to develop energy policies designed to stimulate a coherent pattern of fuel demand, pricing and investment decisions against an appropriate time-table. And some of the most immediate decisions required—for example those relating to nuclear reactor policy—

pertain to those energy sources whose contribution is the most remote in time.

If the world were one country, this type of 'managerial' solution would be both necessary and sufficient. But, as we have seen, there is an unequal distribution of energy resources amongst nations, an unequal impact of oil import costs on the fortunes of nations, and a complex interaction between current oil problems and the pre-existing pattern of international relationships. The case of oil has, therefore, demonstrated that the 'managerial solution', while necessary, is insufficient to deal with the problem of adapting to a new era of fuel consumption and production. The Washington Conference illustrated the conviction of the majority of its participants that a broad co-operative framework of policy-making was essential to deal with the efficient and equitable supply of energy to industrial nations, with the relations between the former and the oil-exporting nations, and with the relations between both those parties and the oil-importing less developed nations. In other words, an approach rooted in the realities and constraints of international politics had to complement the approach of economics, engineering, and project management. With all this in mind, one question which persists is whether the control which OPEC has come to exert over the terms on which consumers may gain access to OPEC oil is an augury of things to come in the case of other resources. If so, do the comments made here on the need for both 'managerial' and 'international political' solutions to the oil problem also apply to non-oil resources?

As background, it is worth recalling that this is not the first time consumers have been faced by a price- and production-controlling cartel. Several commodities were covered by cartel-like schemes in the 1920s and 1930s, and sensational price rises were recorded in some of those cases. The British rubber control scheme of the 1920s, based on Malaya and Ceylon, at first succeeded as sensationally as OPEC in raising prices. Its very success led, however, to its downfall, since it stimulated investment mainly in what is now Indonesia, which was followed by a price collapse.

The history of the Brazilian attempt to control coffee prices in the 1920s offers another example of failure to maintain artificial control of a market. The Brazilians held down exports, despite a bumper crop in 1927, by building up their stocks, confident that at least 3–4 years of recuperation would be needed before the plantations could support another bumper crop. However, the high prices sustained

P.S.—6*

by export limitations during the 1920s had stimulated replanting, and the young trees proved capable of responding to good weather after only two years. The bumper crop of 1929 thus produced a stockholding requirement beyond the Brazilian Government's financial capacity, and resulted in the sudden collapse of prices.

Significantly, the longer-lived cartels of the 1930s marked an awareness of these earlier failures. Profiting from mistakes of excessive exploitation of consumers, the 1930s producers' associations adopted a more co-operative policy *vis-à-vis* consumers. In some cases, they elected consumer representatives as advisers to their committees; in general, they tried to stabilize prices close to the long-term equilibrium level, rather than to maximize short-term prices without regard to the long-term consequences.

Returning to the present, the copper and bauxite producers, as we have indicated in Chapter 5, differ in several significant respects from the oil producers. The more ready supply of substitutes, the availability of scrap, the greater geographical dispersion of reserves, the differing population and financial characteristics of producer nations and the lack of a strong political focus all argue against an OPEC-type situation developing in those commodities. It has also been pointed out[1] that oil was clearly under-priced before October 1973 in relation to its substitutes, whereas this is much less true of almost all non-fuel minerals, substitution for which involves shorter time lags than in the case of fuels.

'Managerial' techniques would clearly play an important rôle in any adaptive process which might be demanded in relation to non-energy resources. In this context, however, because the problem of depletion of individual resources is not so obtrusive as in the case of fuels, the managerial or technical option pertains more to stock-piling, to the economically prudent substitution of one resource for another, and to the recycling of scrap. All of these steps might be resorted to by importing countries if exporting countries were successful in increasing prices. There is little doubt that together they constitute a very powerful bargaining counter in the hands of industrialized importers, the existence of which, even in prospect, would make it clear to producing countries that the long-run price elasticity of demand for their exports would increase, thus limiting their total return. From the viewpoint of the producers themselves, it would swiftly become evident that their chances of bargaining effectively must depend on their forming a cohesive group, possessing a significant proportion of total productive capacity. Because that objective would be so difficult to achieve, for the reasons given in the previous paragraph, it therefore seems unlikely, on purely economic grounds, that the major consumers of non-fuel resources will be faced with the need to embark upon an adaptive process so extensive or so rapid as that which now confronts them in the case of energy.

That may suffice as an economic judgement. But, here again, the political dimension challenges the certitudes of economic analysis. In the first place, as we have attempted to show, there is a strong ideological foundation for policy shared between the less developed resource exporters. This seems likely, from time to time, to produce political imperatives for action on the part of individual exporters or exporters' associations which will over-ride any rational calculation of economic interest. The steady growth of their influence or control over the local extractive and processing activities of resource industries will inevitably encourage certain developing resource exporters to suppose that control over the international market for their product is a straightforward extension of policy. Gains or supposed gains by OPEC in this respect will provide material for comparison which may well catalyse local political pressures for action. It is relevant, for instance, that all the major less developed tin producers (Bolivia, China, Indonesia, Malaysia, and Nigeria) are also producers of oil. In those countries, it will be impossible completely to divorce the policy criteria for the two resources. In the second place, for all non-fuel resources, the delay before consumers are able to accommodate to price rises and/or supply restrictions, while less than that which obtains for oil, is nonetheless a matter of more than a few months. In addition to political motives, there is thus a corresponding opportunity for short-term action by exporters which will not attract immediate retribution.

What we have in mind is that, whenever a grievance, real or imaginary, provides a focus for political solidarity on the part of even the 'weak' resource exporters, as apparently took place in CIPEC during the Kennecott incident described in Chapter 5, underlying bitterness may find expression in effective, if short-term, economic aggression. There could, for example, be selective embargoes of supplies, or brief but disruptive 'campaigns' across a variety of economic, trade, and political fronts against one importer, the impact of which would be enhanced if that action coincided, as it might, with the failure of co-operation between importers. Temporarily effective alliances between resource exporters might be created for just this purpose. Such economic aggression may, moreover, be provoked not only by specific incidents, as in the Kennecott case, but, more generally, by the emergence of a certain type of more effective leadership during a period of rising self-confidence in parts of the Third World.[2]

With possibilities such as these in mind, the 'managerial' solution is seen to be insufficient to deal not only with the problems of fuel but also with plausible actions by non-oil exporters. Despite their inherent long-term weakness, the latter do possess a short-term strength which could be articulated by political considerations, and which conversely, can be countered effectively only by political responses.

The industrial nations must therefore resist the impression that purely 'managerial' policies, whether implemented individually or in concert, can combine with the endemic weakness of non-fuel resource exporter associations to preserve them from the harmful effects of plausible exporter action. A 'managerial' solution, while clearly necessary, will not in itself constitute an appropriate *reply* to the aspirations of Third World exporters of non-fuel resources, just as it will be manifestly insufficient to deal with the oil exporters. Unless there is created a climate of co-operation between resource importers and resource exporters, both 'stronger' and 'weaker', there is danger not only of political acerbity in their relations but also of economic damage, even if only of a short-term character, to the interests of industrialized countries.

The issue for the two principal groups of actors in the resource drama, industrial importers and developing exporters is, then, a very broad one; it is nothing less than the problem of developing a harmonious basis for the joint management of an asymmetrical economic interdependence. Further, that problem extends to working out the ground rules for this relationship in a comparatively short time—before Third World attitudes harden and extreme policies are tried out, and before the impetus of consumer co-operation on energy is lost. While facing the formidable task of adjusting economically to a new energy era, therefore, the industrial countries also have this wider context of international relations to resolve within roughly the same short period.

We argued in Chapter 6 that the industrialized resource importers are at a point of transition in their relationship with the suppliers of resources, and that the future direction of their policies hangs in the balance. Our analysis of the resource policy of the 'independents' in Chapter 7 gave little comfort to importers seeking 'safe areas': that is to say compliant sources of supply outside the developing countries. At the same time it is only the United States which has been seen to have the option of developing long-term supplies of a broad range of resources from indigenous reserves. Therefore, most industrial nations have no choice but to adopt a policy of enhancing the security of supplies from developing exporters, within either a bilateral or a multilateral framework.

In the case of oil, the Washington Conference revealed a qualified consensus in favour of a multilateral format. To any suggestion that this may serve as a general precedent, it may be objected that the 1973/74 oil crisis involved international economic and political problems which necessarily require a multinational political response, to a much deeper and wider extent than is likely to apply in the context of other commodities. It is true that, in a situation of restricted supply of non-oil raw materials, individual importing nations will be affected in a much less homogeneous way than they were by the oil crisis. Their responses will thus be expressed much more naturally in terms of the perceived threat to separate national interests and of the steps to be taken as individual nations to meet the problem. All this seems to point away from a multilateral, co-operative framework of policy. And yet, the example of the particular co-operative arrangements for oil set in train by the Washington Conference is likely to be in existence for some time. Provided that these arrangements do not conspicuously fail, they may well encourage a general disposition to arrange other commodity problems under Washington-type procedures. This would not necessarily rule out bilateral arrangements between some suppliers and some importers, but it would imply that these would be implemented only under implicit or explicit rules of conduct, whereby the effect of such arrangements on the predicament of other importers would be taken into consideration.

The United Nations General Assembly Special Session on raw materials of April 1974 has provided some evidence that the enormity of the resources problem is beginning to be appreciated by the developed nations. This book has mentioned, without analysing, some of the institutional forms of co-operation and action which already exist in the developed world. There is, indeed, ample material for a separate study of present and potential institutions. As an interim contribution to such a study, it seems to us, however, that the institutions which currently exist—the European Community, the multinational companies, the United Nations and the rest—will be, for better or worse, and with no more than minor exceptions, the only institutions which can be relied upon to contribute during this critical period to solving the political and economic problems of adaptation to a new resource era. This is not the time for merely striking attitudes towards these bodies; they are tools with certain capacities which should be used to the fullest extent possible.

There is no doubt that the vital process of accommodation between rich importers and developing exporters will be a difficult one. The problems arising in this process may be either eased or compounded by the oblique entry into the arena of those nations in the categories we have termed 'the independents' and 'the poor'. Unanswered questions abound in this area. Will Canada be able truly to assert a resource policy independent of that of the United States, or are the linkages too numerous and too intense to permit this? Will the Soviet Union and China, acting separately, find it possible to acquire Japanese technology in return for the resources which Japan would prefer to receive from both, or will their mutual suspicion cause a stalemate in which Japan turns perhaps even more strongly to the remaining independent—Australia? Will any of the above-mentioned 'independents' feel obliged to identify more closely with the developing resource exporters than with the industrial nations? In all of this, it is difficult to see how the pressing problems of the resource-deficient developing nations—'the poor'— are to be given adequate prominence amidst the claims and counter-claims of those who are better placed. Nor should it be forgotten that those who take part in attempted OPEC-type cartels in commodities which they produce may well suffer from the effects of similar cartels in commodities which they import.

In the end, we believe that there must be an underlying political basis for constructive reciprocal relations between the proprietors of resources and the proprietors of markets and technology. But market forces will not alone be sufficient to bring about such harmony. The resource producers must be encouraged and enabled to *feel* part of the world system. In industrial economies, important investment decisions are not taken by computer, despite the mythology to the contrary; the sense of confidence and 'rightness' plays a vital rôle. So also, in the developing exporter nations, the feeling of having a genuine commitment to the rest of the world is necessary. Perhaps it is here that the plight of the worst-placed countries may act as a catalyst which brings together all the other actors involved. If a practical programme of action to ease their situation can be evolved co-operatively between all other nations—a target which seems to have emerged from the United Nations Special Session on raw materials—then there will be new grounds for hoping that constructive relations of global interdependence may yet be achieved.

Notes

1. B. Varon and K. Takeuchi, 'Developing Countries and Non-Fuel Minerals', *Foreign Affairs*, April 1974.

2. A 'pessimistic' scenario along these lines is developed in C. Fred Bergsten, 'The Threat from the Third World', *Foreign Policy*, Summer 1973.

Appendix A

Profiles of the Major Mineral Resources

Aluminium

Aluminium is the most abundant metal in the earth's crust, and combines lightness, strength and conductivity. The principal raw material used in obtaining aluminium is bauxite, which is converted to alumina before the latter is in turn reduced by electrolysis to primary aluminium.

Secondary aluminium (aluminium obtained from recycled scrap) accounts for some 20 per cent of total world consumption, which stood at about 14·2 mn tonnes in 1972.

Aluminium consumption has grown at an average rate of 9 per cent per annum over the period 1950–72, although this rate has fallen to 8·4 per cent per annum over the last 10 years.

The world's largest producers of bauxite are Jamaica and Australia (each producing 19 per cent of the total output), Surinam (10 per cent), the Soviet Union (9 per cent), and Guyana (6 per cent). The pattern of primary aluminium production is rather different, as energy costs play an important part in determining the location of smelters. The United States is the world's largest producer, with 33 per cent of the total; other large producers are the Soviet Union (16 per cent), Canada (9 per cent), Japan (8 per cent), and Norway (5 per cent).

Among the large consumers of aluminium, Western Europe has the highest degree of self-sufficiency[1] (41 per cent), owing to the large production of bauxite in Greece and France. Japan and the U.S. are much more dependent on foreign sources of supply, being only 34 per cent and 15 per cent self-sufficient, respectively.

The main uses of aluminium are construction (26 per cent in the U.S.), transportation (19 per cent), containers and packaging (16 per cent) and electrical uses (13 per cent). By far the fastest growth over the past ten years (15 per cent per annum) has occurred in the packaging sector, with electrical and construction uses expanding more or less at the same rate as total consumption.

Copper

Copper, though much less abundant than aluminium, has been extracted and used by man for millennia. Its main properties are thermal and electrical conductivity; its main drawback (apart from price) is its weight (about three times that of aluminium). Most copper is first smelted to produce 'blister', which is then refined electrolytically to produce pure copper.

About 35 per cent of the world's consumption of copper—which stood at 10·7 mn tonnes in 1972—is derived from secondary sources, in the form of both re-refined copper and material used directly.

Consumption of copper has grown at an average annual rate of 4·4 per cent over the period 1950–72; this rate has dropped slightly—to 4·2 per cent in the 1962–72 period.

Mine production of copper derives principally from the U.S. (21 per cent of the total), the Soviet Union (15 per cent), Chile, Zambia (both 10 per cent), and Zaïre (6 per cent). The last three countries, together with Peru, have formed an association known as CIPEC, to uphold their interest as the world's major copper-exporters (see Chapter 5).

Because of its large domestic production and secondary industry, the U.S. is by far the most self-sufficient (91 per cent) of the consuming regions. Western Europe only supplies 28 per cent of its own copper requirements, while in Japan the figure is even lower (23 per cent).

About 40 per cent of copper consumption goes into electrical and electronic uses, while construction takes 23 per cent and industrial machinery and equipment 14 per cent. The other principal users of copper are the transportation and consumer durable sectors.

Iron and Steel

Steel is an iron-based alloy consisting mainly of iron, together with a small amount of carbon, which gives it extra hardness. When other metals (the most important being chromium, nickel, and manganese) are added to steel, its resistance to heat, wear, rust, etc., is increased.

World production of raw steel in 1972 amounted to 628 mn tonnes, about 34 per cent of which derived from recycled scrap.

World consumption of steel rose at an average annual rate of just under 5 per cent during the 1960–72 period. This global figure conceals marked regional disparities; U.S. consumption grew at only 2·5 per cent per annum, whilst that of Japan grew at over 12 per cent.

The Soviet Union is the world's largest producer of iron ore (28 per cent on a contained iron basis); other large producers are the U.S. (12 per cent), Australia (8 per cent), Canada (6 per cent), China and Sweden (each accounting for 5 per cent). The pattern of raw steel output is rather different, owing to the enormous amount of trade in iron ore. The Soviet Union and U.S. each produce 20 per cent of the total, while Japan produces 15 per cent; next in order of importance comes West Germany with 7 per cent, followed by the U.K., France, and China, each with about 4 per cent of world production. These percentages give a fair indication of the relative consumption levels of the various regions, except in the case of Japan, which exports 35 per cent of its production, largely in the form of rolled steel products, to a large number of destinations, including the U.S., China, Canada and many developing countries, whose demand for steel is growing rapidly.

Of the major consuming areas, the U.S. is 75 per cent self-sufficient in the sense described above: its chief sources of imported iron ore are South America and Canada, while it also imports steel products from Japan, Western Europe, and Canada. Western Europe, which is 86 per cent self-sufficient, imports its additional requirements of iron ore from South America (Brazil in particular) and Africa. Japan, by contrast, must import almost all its iron ore (and some scrap), and is only 27 per cent self-sufficient. Its main sources of iron ore are Australia, India, and South America, while it imports scrap from the U.S.

Steel is by far the cheapest metal possessing solidity and strength, and is therefore used in a multitude of applications. The most important of these are construction and transport (each accounting for 25 per cent of the total), and industrial and agricultural machinery (18 per cent). Steel consumption grows most rapidly in industrializing economies which are building up their infrastructure; conversely, there is a saturation level (which the U.S. may have reached) beyond which steel consumption grows at—or even below—the growth-rate of the economy as a whole.

Oil

Oil provides a large and growing proportion of the world's energy demand. This proportion rose from 27·2 per cent in 1951–55, to 47·4 per cent in 1972. Oil fields are found in similar geological formations around the world, but the largest concentrations are in the Middle East (including North Africa) which has some 60 per cent of proven oil reserves. Despite the recent successes of oil explorations in areas like the North Sea, geologists doubt whether there are new 'Middle Easts' awaiting discovery. Crude oil is refined into a wide range of petroleum products. These can also be refined from other sources, such as shale, natural tar sands, and even ordinary bituminous coal. This process usually involves an intermediate stage of synthetic crude ('syncrude') which can be treated at a refinery as an ordinary crude oil. These new sources are currently relatively expensive.

Oil consumption has been growing at 7·5–8 per cent per annum over the last 10 years, but trade in oil has increased at 10·5–11·5 per cent per annum owing mainly to the increased dependence of the U.S. on imports.

The largest oil producer is still the United States with 20 per cent of the total. Other major producers are the Soviet Union (15 per cent), Saudia Arabia (11 per cent), Iran (10 per cent) Venezuela (7 per cent), Kuwait (6 per cent), and Libya (4 per cent). The Middle East a a whole produces 34 per cent of the total.

The United States is the world's largest consumer with 30 per cent of the total. It also has a far greater degree of self-sufficiency (69 per cent) than the other major consuming areas. Western Europe is 3 per cent self-sufficient while Japan imports its entire requirement.

Oil is used for heating, electricity generation and for fuelling engines of all kinds. In some areas it competes with solid fuels, but in the transport sector there is a technical dependence on oil. Oil's competitive strength elsewhere is based on its cheapness, and the ease of extraction and distribution.

Natural Gas

Natural gas is generally found together with oil or in geological formations similar to those holding oil, since it is a product of the same slow process of decay of ancient vegetable and animal remains as crude oil, and a synthetic form of this fossil gas can be produced during the refining of oil. Gas needs more complex and more expensive storage and distribution equipment than oil, and for this reason the world market has so far been less fully developed. In remote oil fields not served by pipelines or other suitable transport facilities natural gas is vented or burnt off as waste product. Natural gas is most widely used in the U.S. where it meets about one-third of energy demand.

Large gas fields in Europe, notably in the Netherlands and under the North Sea, are ideally placed for efficient utilization, near to densely populated areas which can support 'gas grid' pipelines. Imported and locally produced natural gas in Europe now meets about 10 per cent of energy demand, but in the near future it is likely to become proportionally as important as in the U.S.

Improvements in the techniques of liquefaction of natural gas and the shipping of gas will make it possible to reach more distant markets from the gasfields. The high thermal value of natural gas (it contains more than twice the potential heat energy per cubic foot of ordinary manufactured coal gas) and its clean, non-polluting characteristics are prompting a rapid growth in trade.

Coal

Coal, anthracite, lignite ('brown coal'), and peat were the first fossil fuels to be exploited. Although solid fuels are now overshadowed by oil, particularly in the most industrialized countries, they are still major sources of energy, and currently supply about a third of the world's needs. Known reserves of coal are very large indeed, and many areas of the world (notably in Asia) have only been explored in a rudimentary fashion. Engineers have scarcely begun to measure deposits of the lowest grade solid fuel, peat, which is probably also the most widespread.

Coal consumption has been increasing at 2·5 per cent per annum since the early fifties. The major producers of coal are the United States (21 per cent), the Soviet Union (20 per cent); and China (15 per cent). Many other countries produce significant quantities including the United Kingdom, the two Germanies, and Poland.

The United States is a net exporter of coal, about half of which goes to Japan. Western Europe is 83 per cent self-sufficient, partly thanks to government protection, the main imports being made by West Germany and France. Japan relies to a larger extent on imports, being only 35 per cent self-sufficient. Most trade in coal is of 'coking' coal used in blast furnaces for ore reduction.

The declining position of coal in the energy market is mainly due to the fact that it is more expensive to exploit, distribute, and store than oil, and also to the relatively rapid growth of the transport sector where it cannot efficiently be used.

Notes

1. Indigenous mine production plus scrap arisings as a proportion of total consumption.

Appendix B

U.S. Reserves and Resources of Selected Mineral Commodities

Commodity	Units[1]	Probable cumulative primary mineral demand 1971–2000[2]	Reserves at 1971 prices[2]	Identified resources[3]	Hypothetical resources[4]
Aluminium	Million S.T.	370	13	Very large	KDI
Antimony	Thousand S.T.	822	110	Small	Small
Arsenic	Thousand S.T.	800	700	—	—
Asbestos	Million S.T.	43	9	Small	Insignificant
Barium	Million S.T.	31	45	Very large	Very large
Beryllium	Thousand S.T.	28	28	Very large	Huge
Bismuth	Million lb.	81	10	—	—
Boron	Million S.T.	5	40	Very large	Huge
Bromine	Billion lb.	12	17	Huge	Huge
Calcium	Billion S.T.	5	Adequate	Very large	Huge
Cadmium	Million lb.	560	264	—	—
Cesium	Thousand lb.	350	—	—	—
Chlorine	Million S.T.	645	Adequate	Huge	Huge
Chromium	Million S.T.	19	—	Insignificant	Insignificant
Clay	Billion S.T.	3	Adequate	Large	Very large
Coal	Billion S.T.	21	Adequate	Huge	Huge
Cobalt	Million lb.	540	56	—	—
Columbium	Million lb.	288	—	—	—
Construction Stone:					
Crushed	Billion S.T.	41	Adequate	Large	KDI
Dimension	Million S.T.	79	Adequate	Large	KDI
Copper	Million S.T.	93	81	Large	Large
Diatomite	Million S.T.	29	40	Huge	KDI

Commodity	Units[1]	Probable cumulative primary mineral demand 1971–2000[2]	Reserves at 1971 prices[2]	Identified resources[3]	Hypothetical resources[4]
Feldspar	Million L.T.	38	500	Huge	Huge
Fluorine	Million S.T.	39	6	Small	Small
Gallium	Thousand kg.	281	Adequate	—	—
Germanium	Thousand lb.	1,600	900	—	KDI
Gold	Million tr. oz.	293	82	Large	KDI
Graphite	Million S.T.	2	—	Very large	Huge
Gypsum	Million S.T.	726	350	Huge	—
Hafnium	Short Tons	1,280	—	—	—
Indium	Million tr. oz.	19	Adequate	—	—
Iodine	Million lb.	269	11	Very large	Huge
Iron	Billion S.T.	3	225	Very large	Huge
Kyanite	Million S.T.	9	2	Huge	Huge
Lead	Million S.T.	34	15	Large	Moderate
Limestone and Dolomite	—	—	17	Large	KDI
Lithium	Thousand S.T.	183	—	Huge	Huge
Magnesium	Million S.T.	52	2,767	Huge	Huge
Manganese	Million S.T.	50	Adequate	Large	KDI
Mercury	Thousand flasks[5]	1,730	—	Small	KDI
Mica, sheet	Million lb.	62	75	Insignificant	Very large
Mica, scrap and flakes	Million S.T.	7	250	Huge	Huge
Molybdenum	Billion lb.	3	6	Huge	Huge
Natural Gas	Trillion cu. ft.	1,098	279[6]	Moderate	Large
Nickel	Billion lb.	14	—	Large	KDI
Nitrogen	Million S.T.	1,018	Adequate	Huge	Huge
Peat	Million S.T.	43	Adequate	Huge	KDI
Petroleum	Billion bbls.	276	38	Large	Large
Phosphorus	Million S.T.	208	39	Very large	Huge
Planinum	Million tr. oz.	16	1	Moderate	Large
Potassium	Million S.T.	216	50	Very large	Huge
Pumice	Million S.T.	208	200	—	—

Rare earths	Thousand S.T.	452	5,045	Huge	KDI
Rhenium	Thousand lb.	360	400	—	—
Sodium	Million S.T.	1,160	Adequate	Huge	Huge
Sand and Gravel	Billion S.T.	54	Adequate	Large	KDI
Scandium	kg.	554	Adequate	—	—
Silver	Million tr. oz.	4,400	1,300	Moderate	Large
Strontium	Thousand S.T.	771	75	Huge	Huge
Sulphur	Million L.T.	514	150	Huge	Huge
Talc	Million S.T.	52	—	Very large	Huge
Thorium	Thousand S.T.	21	2	Very large	KDI
Titanium	Million S.T.	32	33	Very large	Very large
Tungsten	Million lb.	1,000	175	Moderate	Moderate
Uranium	Thousand S.T.	1,240	130	Very large	Large
Vanadium	Thousand S.T.	471	115	Large	KDI
Zinc	Million S.T.	62	30	Very large	Very large
Zirconium	Million S.T.	4	4	Large	KDI

NOTES AND DEFINITIONS:

1. S.T. = Short tons. L.T. = Long tons. lb. = pounds. tr. oz. = troy ounces. kg. = kilograms. bbl = 42 gallons.
2. As estimated by U.S. Bureau of Mines, 1973.   3. Identified Resources are defined as including reserves and materials other than reserves which are essentially well known as to location, extent, and grade and which may be exploitable in the future under more favourable economic conditions or with improvements in technology.
4. Hypothetical resources are undiscovered, but geologically predictable, deposits of materials similar to identified resources.
5. 76 lbs. Flasks.   6. Less than one unit.

RESOURCE APPRAISAL TERMS:

Huge: Domestic resources (of the category shown) are greater than ten times the minimum anticipated cumulative demand (MACD) between the years 1971 and 2000.
Very large: Domestic resources are two to ten times the MACD.
Large: Domestic resources are approximately 75 per cent to twice the MACD.
Moderate: Domestic resources are approximately 35 per cent to 75 per cent of the MACD.
Small: Domestic resources are approximately 10 per cent to 35 per cent of the MACD.
Insignificant: Domestic resources are less than 10 per cent of the MACD.
KDI: (Known Data Insufficient)—Resources not estimated because of insufficient geological knowledge of surface or subsurface area.

—Dashes indicate data not available.

Source: Material Needs and the Environment Today and Tomorrow, Final Report of the National Commission on Materials Policy, June 1973.

Bibliography

Books

BARNETT, H. J. & MORSE, C.: *Scarcity and Growth*, Johns Hopkins for Resources for the Future, Inc., Baltimore, 1963.

CLAWSON, MARION (editor): *Natural Resources and International Development*, Johns Hopkins for Resources for the Future, Inc., 1964.

COLE, H. S. D., *et al.* (editors): *Thinking about the Future—A Critique of 'The Limits to Growth'*, Science Policy Research Unit, University of Sussex, Chatto & Windus/Sussex University Press, 1973.

FISHER, J. L. & POTTER, N.: *World Prospects for Natural Resources*, Johns Hopkins for Resources for the Future, Inc., 1974.

LANDSBERG, H. H. *et al.*: *Resources in America's Future*, Johns Hopkins for Resources for the Future, Inc., 1964.

MEADOWS, D. H. *et al.*: *The Limits to Growth: A Report for the Club of Rome's Project on the Predicament of Man*, Washington and London, 1972.

The National Commission on Materials Policy: *Material Needs and the Environment Today and Tomorrow*, Washington, 1973.

Resources and Man, Committee on: *Resources and Man*, National Academy of Sciences, and National Research Council, San Francisco, 1969.

SUTULOV, A.: *Minerals in World Affairs*, University of Utah, 1972.

TURNER, L.: *Multinational Companies and the Third World*, Allen Lane, London, 1974.

ZIMMERMANN, E.: *Introduction to World Resources*, New York, 1964.

Articles

BERGSTEN, C. F.: 'The Threat from the Third World', *Foreign Policy*, Summer 1973.

Business Week: 'The Scramble for Resources', 30 June 1973.

HOTELLING, H.: 'The Economics of Exhaustible Resources', *Journal of Political Economy*, April 1931.

MADDOX, J.: 'Raw Materials and the Price Mechanism', *Nature*, 14 May 1972.

MERO, J. L.: 'Oceanic Mineral Resources', *Futures*, April 1969.

POSNER, M. V.: 'The Rate of Depletion of Gas Fields', *Economic Journal*, March 1972.

Science Policy Research Unit, University of Sussex: 'The Limits to Growth Controversy', *Futures*, April 1973.

VARON, B. & TAKEUCHI, K.: 'Developing Countries and Non-Fuel Minerals', *Foreign Affairs*, April 1974.

Index